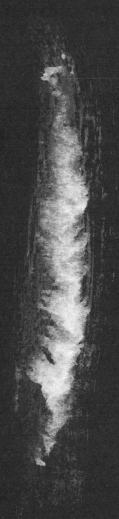

PENGUIN BOOKS
UK I USA I Canada I Ireland I Australia
India I New Zealand I South Africa

Penguin Books is part of the Penguin Random House group of companies
whose addresses can be found at global.penguinrandomhouse.com.

www.penguin.co.uk   www.puffin.co.uk   www.ladybird.co.uk

Penguin
Random House
UK

First published 2018
001

Written by Alasdair Cullen, Jack Harry, Gaby Kirschner, Eli Mengem, Cavan Scott,
Martino Simcik, Neil Stacey, Lawrence Tallis
Project Director: Soraya Rowley
Copyright © Copa90 Ltd, 2018

Illustrations by Kevin McGivern
Illustrations copyright © Kevin McGivern, 2018
Photography credits on page 176
Designed by Andy Archer

Printed in China

A CIP catalogue record for this book is available from the British Library

ISBN: 978–0–141–38772–7

All correspondence to:
Penguin Books
Penguin Random House Children's
80 Strand, London WC2R 0RL

MIX
Paper from
responsible sources
FSC
www.fsc.org
FSC® C018179

COPA90

OUR WORLD CUP
A FANS'
GUIDE TO
2018

PENGUIN BOOKS

CONTENTS

8 THE GREATEST SHOW ON EARTH

10 HOW THE WORLD CUP TAUGHT US TO PLAY

12 A SHORT HISTORY OF THE WORLD CUP

14 THE WORLD CUP BY NUMBERS

18 GROUP A

30 RUSSIA'S WORLD CUP JOURNEY

32 RUSSIAN FOOTBALL HIGHS AND LOWS

34 RUSSIA'S FAVOURITE SON

36 GROUP B

48 OUR RUSSIA

56 GROUP C

68 QUALIFIER STORIES

76 GROUP D

88 EPIC UNDERDOGS

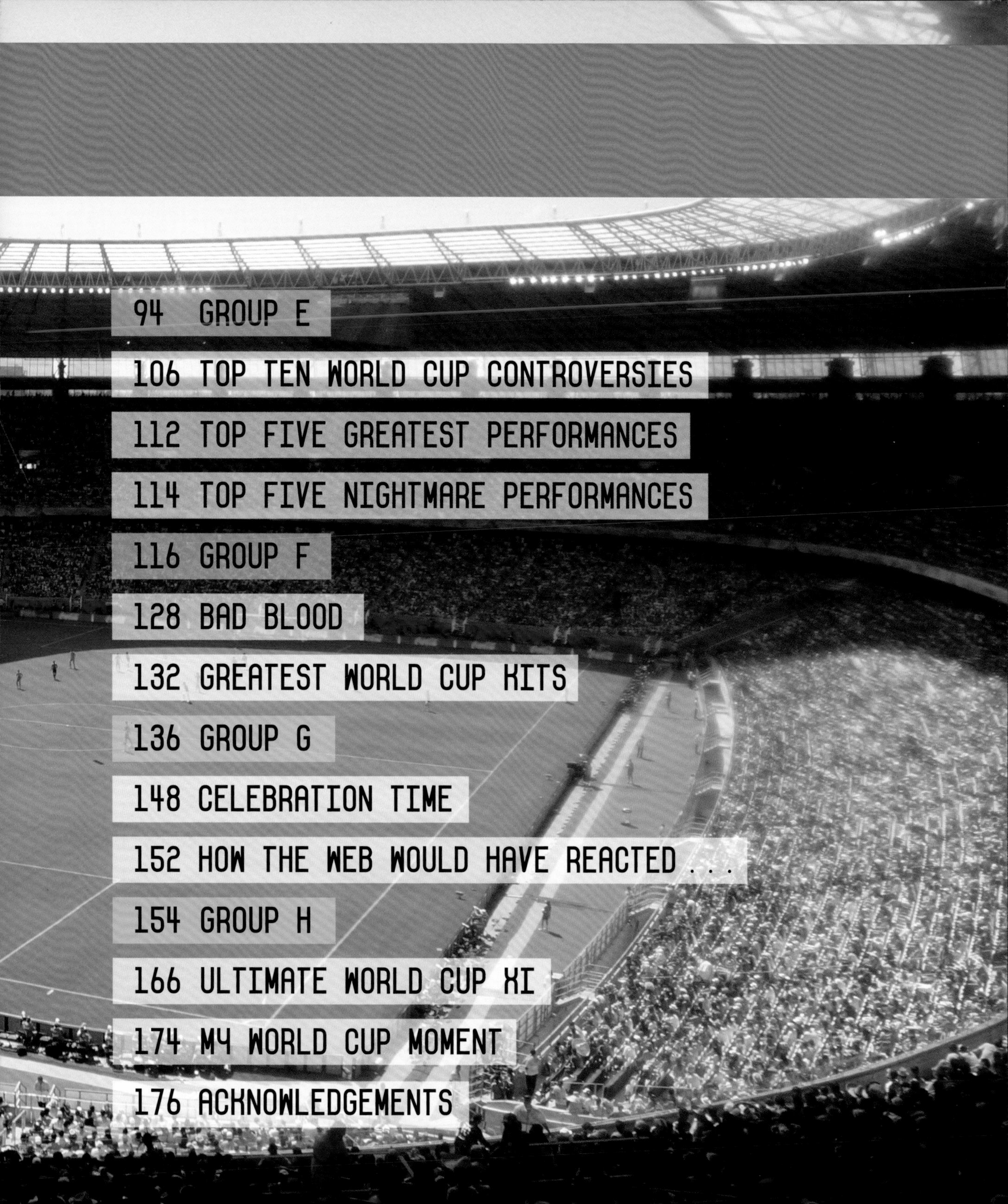

94 GROUP E

106 TOP TEN WORLD CUP CONTROVERSIES

112 TOP FIVE GREATEST PERFORMANCES

114 TOP FIVE NIGHTMARE PERFORMANCES

116 GROUP F

128 BAD BLOOD

132 GREATEST WORLD CUP KITS

136 GROUP G

148 CELEBRATION TIME

152 HOW THE WEB WOULD HAVE REACTED . . .

154 GROUP H

166 ULTIMATE WORLD CUP XI

174 MY WORLD CUP MOMENT

176 ACKNOWLEDGEMENTS

◀ All the passion and colour of the World Cup – before the World Cup has even started. Peru fans create an electric atmosphere as their nation draws 1–1 with Colombia to progress to a qualification play-off against New Zealand.

THE GREATEST SHOW ON EARTH

Its history, drama and passion are unmatchable. It dwarfs the Super Bowl, World Series and Olympics combined. It's the only tournament to have started a war, and the only tournament to have stopped a war.* It is, of course, the World Cup.

In 2014, 32 of the planet's best international teams came together in Brazil to create a festival of football. Some aimed to lift the trophy. Others were given no hope. But all 736 players were there to live that same childhood dream of running out onto the pitch at the game's number one event.

And then there's us: the fans. The last World Cup final, between Germany and Argentina in 2014, was watched by over one billion people. That's 14 per cent of the planet's entire population, stopping what they're doing to watch a small patch of grass in Rio de Janeiro for 90 minutes (plus extra-time!). From villages in Togo to skyscrapers in Tokyo, our love of the beautiful game brought the globe shuddering to a standstill.

That concluding, showpiece match was just the tip of the iceberg. The total number of viewers for the 2014 tournament came to a jaw-dropping 25 billion.

Away from TV, the tournament brought Brazil more than a million visitors, tripling the country's tourism average for that time of year. And a combined total of nearly three and a half million lucky fans somehow squeezed into 12 stadiums to watch the games in person.

Now, in 2018, as the world's focus shifts to Russia, the competition's popularity remains the same. The World Cup stands alone, unrivalled, as the only tournament truly deserving of the title 'The Greatest Show on Earth'.

*To find out all about this, head to page 68.

THREE TIMES THE WORLD CUP WENT BEYOND THE PITCH

1 Thousands took to the streets of the Senegalese capital, Dakar, after Senegal's surprise victory over France in the opening match of Japan/Korea 2002. Amid the celebrations, President Abdoulaye Wade held a football aloft and declared the day a national holiday.

2 There were even bigger parties in Seoul, South Korea's capital, when the Reds made it to the semi-finals on home turf in 2002. Three million people went outside to celebrate, but the real shock was that even the chairman of North Korea's FA wrote to his South Korean counterpart to offer his congratulations. Why is that such a big deal? The two nations are long-standing enemies and the letter came just a day after a conflict between the two.

3 In Argentina, the *Iglesia Maradoniana* – which translates as the 'Church of Maradona' – is a real-life thing. Created in honour of the man whose breath-taking (but controversial) performances at Mexico 1986 brought the nation its second World Cup triumph, it's an officially recognized religion with over 150,000 members.

▲ Germany's Mario Götze scores the only goal of the 2014 World Cup final – and is instantly immortalized in football history.

HOW THE WORLD CUP TAUGHT US TO PLAY

Before leagues across the world could be watched from the comfort of your own home, the World Cup was the one true chance for countries to showcase their distinct footballing philosophies. Here are four styles that were popularized at the World Cup.

Italian football has been characterized by *Il Catenaccio* ('The Chain'), a defensive style seeking to take advantage of opponents on the counter. On home soil in 1990, coach Azeglio Vicini used it to lead Italy all the way to the semi-finals, incredibly conceding just one goal along the way.

England has traditionally used physicality to make the most of 50/50 challenges against defenders – sometimes with success (1966) and sometimes not (most other World Cups since!).

The **Dutch** were major advocates of Total Football, in which players switch quickly into other positions. For a masterclass, look no further than the Johan Cruyff-inspired side of the 1974 World Cup.

Brazilian sides have often used highly technical players to break down defences and widen play through a superior midfield. With players like Pelé, Jairzinho and Rivellino at their disposal, Brazil's class of 1970 used this style to become arguably the most devastating football team there ever was.

Today, many of the game's biggest stars play their club football away from their own national leagues, and once-distinctive styles of play have merged into one. However, you can always expect a few surprises at the World Cup.

A SHORT HISTORY

1930

In 1930, nearly 80 years after the rules of football were officially written, the first football World Cup was both hosted and won by Uruguay. Thirteen teams from three continents took part.

1934–38

The 1934 and 1938 World Cups were held in Italy and France respectively. The former introduced the 16-team format (which remained fixed until 1982). Both were won by Italy who, due to the outbreak of the Second World War (1939–45), would remain unchallenged holders for the next 12 years.

1950–54

The World Cup eventually returned with the Brazil tournament in 1950. Uruguay won, dramatically defeating the hosts in front of 200,000 home fans in the Maracanã stadium. Four years later, West Germany were the winners in Switzerland.

1986

Mexico hosted for a second time in 1986. Diego Maradona lit up the tournament and scored two iconic quarter-final goals against England, before Argentina marched on to a victorious final.

▲ Uruguay's class of 1930, hosts and winners of the first-ever World Cup.

1994

The tournament went Stateside for USA 1994, and ended with the first World Cup final to be decided on penalties. Roberto Baggio skied his effort and there was heartbreak for Italy as Brazil won its fourth World Cup.

1990

Italy 1990 was the first 'modern tournament' with broadcasters from all over the world, TV studios in every host city, and nightly chat shows revolving around every match. Cameroon stole people's hearts on their way to becoming the first African side to reach the quarter-finals, but it was West Germany who lifted the trophy.

▲ Salvatore 'Toto' Schillaci was one of the surprise stars of 1990, scoring six goals and winning the Golden Boot.

1998

France 1998 saw the tournament expanded again, this time to 32 teams. The dominant hosts won the prize, with Zinedine Zidane pulling the strings throughout.

2002

The 2002 World Cup was the first to be held in Asia, and also the first to be co-hosted by two nations, Korea and Japan. However, it was Brazil who took the trophy.

2006

Germany hosted a wonderful tournament in 2006. However, it was Italy and France who went all the way to the final, where the Italians won on penalties.

OF THE WORLD CUP

1958–62
In 1958, the world first laid its eyes on Pelé. The 17-year-old's two goals in the final helped Brazil to a 5–2 win over hosts Sweden. It was Brazil's first World Cup triumph, and the first time a nation had won the tournament outside its own continent. The Brazilians would go on to lift the trophy again at Chile 1962.

1966
In 1966 football 'came home'. The English, who stake a claim to having invented the game, were awarded their first World Cup, and with it came a mascot, an anthem, and much of the fanfare that we know and love about the tournament today.

1970
Mexico 1970 saw the end of an era, as Brazil won the Jules Rimet Trophy (the original trophy awarded at the World Cup) for a third time and were permitted to keep it. This was the first tournament to be televised in colour, and also featured the famous 'Game of the Century' in which Italy beat West Germany 4–3 to reach the final.

1978
The 1978 tournament in Argentina was perhaps the most controversial in history. Argentina's rule under military dictatorship caused many, including Johan Cruyff, to boycott the competition. Despite the absence of their star man and captain, the Dutch made it to the final again, but lost 3–1 to the hosts.

1974
The 1974 World Cup in West Germany saw the hosts see off a classy Netherlands side in a memorable final. Many still consider that Dutch side to be the best team to lose a World Cup.

1982
At Spain 1982, the tournament was expanded from 16 to 24 teams. Italy keeper Dino Zoff, aged 40, became the oldest person to lift a World Cup.

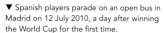

▼ Spanish players parade on an open bus in Madrid on 12 July 2010, a day after winning the World Cup for the first time.

▼ Moscow's spectacular Luzhniki Stadium will host both the opening and closing matches of the 2018 World Cup.

2010
In 2010 the tournament made its first stop in Africa, with South Africa playing host. Spain won its first tournament, handing the Netherlands their third World Cup final defeat.

2014
If football came home in 1966, it returned to its spiritual home in 2014. The World Cup in Brazil was an absolute celebration of football. Despite going out 7–1 to Germany in the semis, the hosts created an electric atmosphere and breathed a collective sigh of relief as their major rival, Argentina, lost out to Germany in the final.

2018
Now the 2018 stage belongs to Russia. It will be the first tournament to be hosted across Europe and Asia, the first to take place in 11 host cities, and will feature the longest distances between matches in World Cup history.

THE WORLD CUP BY NUMBERS

So you think you know your World Cup trivia? Here are 23 of our favourite facts – one for each shirt number in a World Cup squad.

José Batista holds the not-so-proud record for the fastest red card in World Cup history. Batista saw red for scything down Gordon Strachan after less than **one** minute (56 seconds, to be precise) of Uruguay's 1986 match against Scotland. Despite playing with ten men for 89 minutes, Batista's teammates were able to hold on for a 0–0 draw.

The World Cup trophy has been stolen on **two** occasions. In 1966, it was taken from a public exhibition in London, but famously found a week later by a dog named Pickles. After winning the Cup for a third time in 1970, Brazil were allowed to keep the trophy – but in 1983 it was taken from their Federation offices, never to be found again.

Bert Patenaude was the first player to score a World Cup hat-trick, netting all **three** of the USA's goals in a 3–0 win over Paraguay in 1930.

Mexican Rafael Márquez became the first captain to lead his country out in **four** separate World Cup tournaments (2002–14).

Russian striker Oleg Salenko holds the record for most goals scored in a single World Cup match. In 1994, during a group game against Cameroon, Salenko scored the first **five** Russian goals in a thumping 6–1 win.

Mexico lost a record **nine** consecutive games at the World Cup, spanning the 1930, 1950 and 1958 tournaments.

Six teams have gone unbeaten at a World Cup without being crowned champions. They are:
Scotland in 1974 *(1 win, 2 draws)*
Brazil in 1978 *(4 wins, 3 draws)*
England in 1982 *(3 wins, 2 draws)*
Cameroon in 1982 *(3 draws)*
Belgium in 1998 *(3 draws)*
New Zealand in 2010 *(3 draws)*

Nine months after Germany hosted the World Cup in 2006, the country's birth rate increased by **ten** per cent.

Seven players have won all three possible World Cup medals (winner, runner-up and third place). They are:
Franz Beckenbauer, Jürgen Grabowski, Horst-Dieter Höttges, Sepp Maier and Wolfgang Overath *(all West Germany)*, Miroslav Klose *(Germany)* and Franco Baresi *(Italy)*

It took Hakan Şükür just **11** seconds to score the World Cup's fastest goal, during Turkey's 3–2 win over South Korea in the 2002 third-place play-off match.

Of the 77 countries that have played in the World Cup (not including the 2018 tournament), only **eight** nations have lifted the World Cup trophy. They are:

Uruguay　　　*England*
Italy　　　*Argentina*
(West) Germany　　*France*
Brazil　　　*Spain*

The highest-scoring game in World Cup history was a **12**-goal thriller in 1954, when Austria defeated Switzerland 7–5.

In the 1958 Finals, French striker Just Fontaine claimed the record for most goals scored in a single World Cup tournament. He notched up an incredible **13** goals in just six games.

Norman Whiteside is the youngest player ever to take to the field at a World Cup. He was just **17** years and 41 days old when he played for Northern Ireland at the 1982 World Cup in Spain. Legend has it that on his return home he was grounded for a week by his mum for not calling her to let her know he'd arrived safely in Madrid.

The **2014** World Cup was the first World Cup to have goal-line technology. France's Karim Benzema was the first player to be awarded a goal by technology, in a group game against Honduras.

The first World Cup in 1930 consisted of **18** matches. The 2018 World Cup will feature 64.

15 is the total number of World Cup goals scored by Brazilian legend Ronaldo, a figure topped only by . . .

Lucien Laurent's **19**th-minute goal for France against Mexico in 1930 was the first-ever goal scored at a World Cup.

. . . German striker Miroslav Klose, who holds the record number of goals at **16**. That is also the record number of saves in a single game, a feat achieved by USA's Tim Howard against Belgium in 2014.

Brazil have appeared at the most consecutive World Cups, playing in all **20** tournaments. They'll make it 21 at the 2018 World Cup.

21 Italy's Gianluca Pagliuca was the first goalkeeper ever to get sent off at a World Cup. Pagliuca was red-carded **21** minutes into a match against Norway in 1994. Despite this, Italy still won 1–0.

22 In 20**22**, Qatar will become the smallest country ever to host a World Cup. The previous smallest host, Switzerland, is over three times bigger than the Arab nation.

23-player squads were allowed from the 2002 World Cup onwards. However, the number 23 shirt made an unofficial debut in the 1962 competition, when Uruguay's Guillermo Escalada wore it due to superstition (there was no number 13 in the squad).

COPA90

 RUSSIA

With home advantage on their side and a gigantic population of almost 145 million willing them on, the weight of expectation on Russian shoulders has never been greater. Expect the atmosphere at each of their games to be immense, especially when they take to the pitch for the tournament's opening match against Saudi Arabia at Moscow's iconic Luzhniki Stadium.

WORLD CUP NUMBERS

ATTENDED	10
GAMES PLAYED	40
WIN PERCENTAGE	43%
WORLD CUPS WON	0
MILES TO MOSCOW	0

MOST CAPS 120	MOST GOALS 42
SERGEI IGNASHEVICH	OLEH BLOKHIN

THEIR GREATEST MOMENT
= EURO 1960 FINAL =

This was the first UEFA European Championship (then called the European Nations' Cup), and the Soviet Union were its first winners. A tense final in Paris saw Yugoslavia go 1–0 up, and it took a string of fine saves from that man Yashin to keep the Soviets in the game. A second-half equalizer took the match into extra-time, where a late header from star striker Viktor Ponedelnik proved to be Russian football's crowning moment.

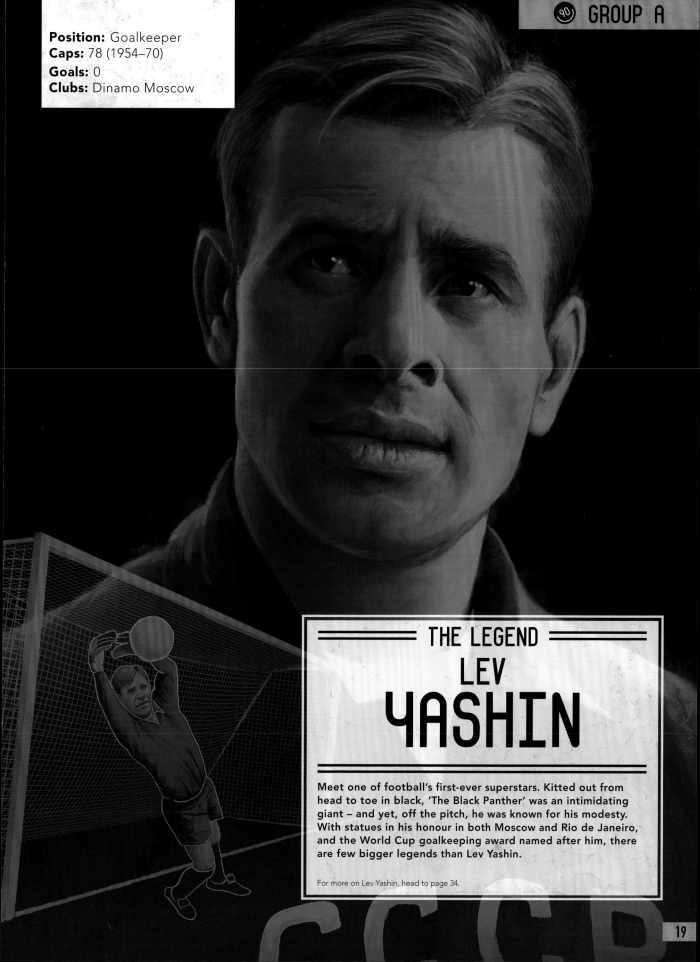

Position: Goalkeeper
Caps: 78 (1954–70)
Goals: 0
Clubs: Dinamo Moscow

THE LEGEND
LEV YASHIN

Meet one of football's first-ever superstars. Kitted out from head to toe in black, 'The Black Panther' was an intimidating giant – and yet, off the pitch, he was known for his modesty. With statues in his honour in both Moscow and Rio de Janeiro, and the World Cup goalkeeping award named after him, there are few bigger legends than Lev Yashin.

For more on Lev Yashin, head to page 34.

★ **THE RISING STAR** ★

ALEKSANDR

GOLOVIN

Nicknamed 'the Russian Ronaldo', CSKA Moscow's creative attacking midfielder played his first professional match in March 2015. Only three months later, he was scoring his first senior international goal. Played out of position as a defensive midfielder at Euro 2016, Golovin struggled to find the net – but pushed forward the 22-year-old is a force to be reckoned with.

DID YOU KNOW?

Football matches in Russia can get seriously cold – below -10°C, in fact. It can make for some interesting playing conditions, as Dinamo Moscow's Zvjezdan Misimović found out when he was bombarded with snowballs by Spartak Moscow fans during a match in 2012. They were getting their own back after he fired a ball into the crowd.

THE RISING STAR ★

FAHAD
AL-MUWALLAD

...-Muwallad deservedly ...ig share of the credit for ...ry's place at the World Cup. ...-footed Al Ittihad winger ...the bench in their final ...g match against Japan to ...e game's only goal and book ...to Russia. He's said to be ...e fastest players in Asia – ...bably explains his ..., 'The Cheetah'.

DID YOU KNOW?

With 178 official international appearances between 1993 and 2006, Saudi Arabia's Mohamed Al-Deayea is the most-capped goalkeeper in the world. He was his country's number one in all four of their previous World Cup appearances.

SAUDI ARABIA

After a 12-year absence from football's biggest tournament, the Green Falcons are back and eager to make an impression. Can they top their USA 1994 performance, when Saeed Al-Owairan scored one of the World Cup's greatest-ever goals en route to a place in the last 16?

WORLD CUP NUMBERS

ATTENDED	4
GAMES PLAYED	13
WIN PERCENTAGE	15%
WORLD CUPS WON	0
MILES TO MOSCOW	2,196

MOST CAPS 🧢 178
MOHAMED AL-DEAYEA

MOST GOALS ⚽ 71
MAJED ABDULLAH

THEIR GREATEST MOMENT

1984 AFC ASIAN CUP

After scraping through to the final of the 1984 Asian Cup on penalties, Saudi Arabia faced China in Singapore. Saudi took a 1–0 lead into the half-time break, but it was what happened in the second half that truly became the stuff of legend. A minute after the restart, Majed Abdullah picked the ball up just inside the Chinese half, danced past two defenders and tricked the keeper with a delightful dummy before slotting home the decisive second goal.

The 2–0 win was the first of three Asian Cup trophies for the Green Falcons.

Position: Forward
Caps: 116 (1977–94)
Goals: 71
Clubs: Al Nassr

THE LEGEND
MAJED
ABDULLAH

Abdullah's goalscoring record is, frankly, frightening. In a 20-year playing career all spent with the same club (Saudi league side Al Nassr), 'The Arabian Jewel' scored an unthinkable 260 goals in 240 matches. On the world stage, his 71 goals in the green and white of Saudi Arabia put him in the top-ten international goalscorers of all time. The World Cup almost eluded him but, at the age of 35, he captained his nation at World Cup 1994 before bowing out of the international game on a high.

EGYPT

Egypt were the first-ever African nation to go to the World Cup, way back in 1934. The 1990 World Cup was their only other appearance since then, but don't let that fool you – they have won the African Cup of Nations a record seven times and come to Russia off the back of being runners-up in the 2017 tournament.

WORLD CUP NUMBERS

ATTENDED	2
GAMES PLAYED	4
WIN PERCENTAGE	0%
WORLD CUPS WON	0
MILES TO MOSCOW	1,798

MOST CAPS	184	MOST GOALS	69
AHMED HASSAN		HOSSAM HASSAN	

THEIR GREATEST MOMENT

1986 AFRICAN CUP OF NATIONS

After winning the first two African Cup of Nations in 1957 and 1959, Egypt didn't lift the trophy for another 27 years. As hosts in 1986, they finally put their barren spell well and truly behind them. After the shock of losing their opening match against Senegal, they recovered to blitz the group stage, knock out Morocco in the semis and take on Cameroon in a tense, goalless final. In front of a crowd of nearly 100,000, they won the penalty shootout, with manager Mike Smith becoming one of the few English coaches to win an international tournament in the process.

Position: Forward
Caps: 169 (1985–2006)
Goals: 69
Clubs: Al Ahly (twice), PAOK, Neuchâtel Xamax, Al Ain, Zamalek, Al Masry, Tersana, Al Ittihad Alexandria

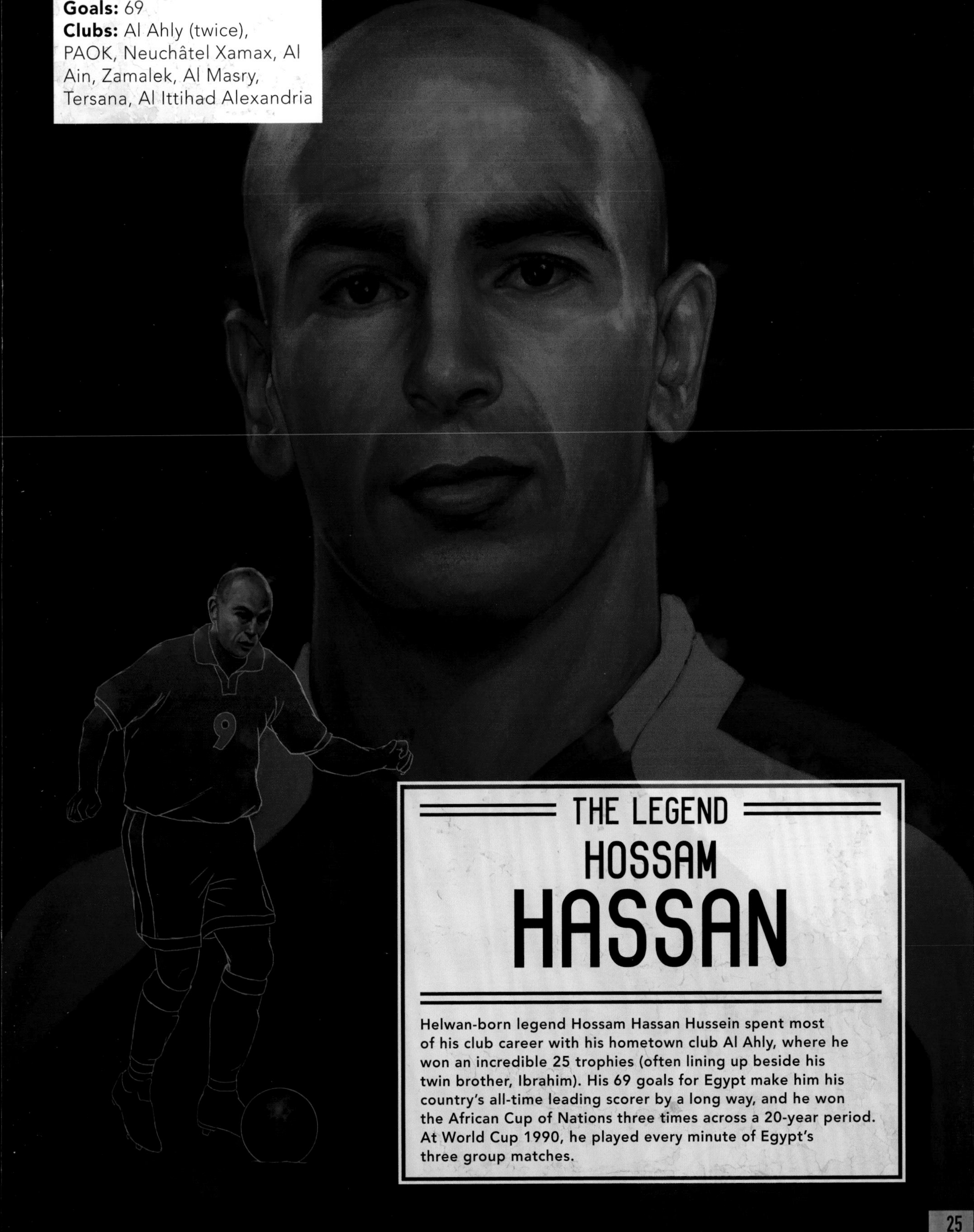

THE LEGEND
HOSSAM
HASSAN

Helwan-born legend Hossam Hassan Hussein spent most of his club career with his hometown club Al Ahly, where he won an incredible 25 trophies (often lining up beside his twin brother, Ibrahim). His 69 goals for Egypt make him his country's all-time leading scorer by a long way, and he won the African Cup of Nations three times across a 20-year period. At World Cup 1990, he played every minute of Egypt's three group matches.

★ **THE RISING STAR** ★

MOHAMED
SALAH

Though he struggled to make an impression at Chelsea, Mo Salah gave his doubters something to think about during a prolific spell at Roma where he netted 29 goals in 65 games. Since then he's made a record-breaking £39 million switch to Liverpool, and scored the 95th-minute penalty against Congo that sent Egypt to Russia. Dangerous coming in from the right wing with his killer left foot, the 25-year-old is swiftly becoming Egypt's talisman.

DID YOU KNOW?

Ahmed Hassan won an astonishing 184 caps for Egypt between 1995 and 2012, making him the most-capped male footballer in history. Despite his efforts, he never got to play at a World Cup.

★ **THE RISING STAR** ★

RODRIGO

BENTANCUR

Having caught the eye as a key player in the Uruguay team that won the South American U-20 Championship in 2017, Bentancur has already broken into the full national side and looks a strong bet to be on the plane to Russia. The versatile midfielder made his name at Boca Juniors, before moving to Italy to join Juventus. A strong passer with either foot, he plays exceptionally well in tight spaces and is capable of blistering runs from behind.

DID YOU KNOW?

Uruguay is the smallest country to have won the World Cup. Its population when it won in 1930 was just 1.75 million, and even today it's only 3.4 million. Even Panama has more people.

URUGUAY

As the World Cup's first-ever hosts and champions, *La Celeste* ('The Sky Blue') have some serious history. More recent years have been less kind to them, but with players like Luis Suárez and Edinson Cavani to call upon, you can never write off Uruguay.

WORLD CUP NUMBERS

ATTENDED	12
GAMES PLAYED	51
WIN PERCENTAGE	39%
WORLD CUPS WON	★★ 2
MILES TO MOSCOW	▶ 8,316

MOST CAPS 123	MOST GOALS 49
MAXI PEREIRA	LUIS SUÁREZ

THEIR GREATEST MOMENT
═ 1930 WORLD CUP ═

For many, Uruguay's incredible performance at the 1950 World Cup will go down as their finest achievement – but as that's well covered elsewhere in this book (see page 89), we're going for that first triumph in 1930. In an inaugural tournament that saw just 13 nations come together, the hosts saw off Peru, Romania, Yugoslavia and finally Argentina to lift the Jules Rimet trophy in front of a jubilant home crowd.

Position: Forward
Caps: 21 (1946–54)
Goals: 8
Clubs: Peñarol, AC Milan, Roma

═ THE LEGEND ═
JUAN ALBERTO
SCHIAFFINO

Joining his brother Raúl at Peñarol at the age of 18, Schiaffino helped the side win the Uruguayan league on four separate occasions. With peerless ball control and over 140 goals to his name, this selfless forward wasn't just about scoring: he also had a knack for picking out a game-changing pass. Unusually, he also played four times for Italy, but it's his performances for Uruguay, with whom he won the 1950 World Cup, for which he's best known.

RUSSIA'S WORLD CUP JOURNEY

▶ The Samara Arena during its hectic construction phase ahead of hosting six matches at the 2018 World Cup.

It's fair to say the last few years haven't been the best for Russian football.

With the national team failing to get beyond the group stages of either the 2014 World Cup or Euro 2016, and losing two of their three matches at 2017's Confederations Cup, there simply hasn't been much to celebrate.

Controversy surrounding the country's successful bid to host the World Cup didn't help to change the negative narrative either. When the decision was announced in December 2010, it seemed impossible that a sprawling, poorly connected country like Russia had defeated bids from England, Spain/Portugal and Belgium/Holland. But,

as Sepp Blatter argued at the time, the World Cup had never been in eastern Europe. It was time to give them the chance to host the world's greatest tournament.

Of course, Russia has hosted major sporting events before. The 2006 Women's U-20 World Championship was held in Moscow and Saint Petersburg and, most famously, the 2014 Winter Olympics in Sochi were a major success. But with the brightest footballing spotlight finally on the region, it gives the country and its Football Union (Russia's FA) the chance to truly showcase its football heritage.

The majority of the grounds being constructed or renovated will be used by Russian clubs after the competition, and Russia's bid also included a commitment to grassroots projects. The Russia team itself could also reap the benefits. As hosts, Russia are of course guaranteed a place at the tournament, and hopes are high that home advantage will help them kick-start their fortunes.

Importantly, the World Cup also gives Russian supporters the chance to disprove their doubters. Violence flared when Russian hooligans travelled to France for Euro 2016, but many fans will be desperate to prove that there is also a friendly, welcoming side to Russia and its football culture. The government is playing its own part in this by increasing security and coming up with a 'black list' of banned troublemakers.

On the pitch and in the stands, the 2018 World Cup gives Russia the opportunity to remind the world

that it is about much more than scandal and shoddy results. It is a country with a rich footballing history and a bright footballing future – jump-starting, they hope, right here.

The hosts' road to the finals has been a rocky one, but now could be their big chance to shine.

WHAT'S IN A NAME?

The host nation has played under a few different names over the years. Brush up on your knowledge with this quick guide . . .

1910–14
A **Russian Empire** side plays 16 matches, including an appearance at the 1912 Olympics – but effectively disbands when the First World War starts.

1924–91
The **Soviet Union** team – also known as the **Union of Soviet Socialist Republics** (**USSR** in English, or **CCCP** in Russian) – is a mainstay of international football.

1992
Following the break-up of the Soviet Union, a **Commonwealth of Independent States** (**CIS**) team is briefly formed in order to play at Euro 1992.

1992 – Present Day
Fifteen new national associations arise from the break-up of the Soviet Union. However, it's **Russia** that is officially recognized as the successor to the Soviet side, inheriting its history and records.

RUSSIAN FOOTBALL

JUL 1960
The high point of Russian football history, as Yashin and co. win the Euros with a 2–1 triumph over Yugoslavia. It remains the Soviet Union/Russia's only major championship victory.

JUL 1966
A best-ever World Cup performance, finishing fourth after losing 2–1 to Portugal in the bronze-medal match.

SEP 1954
Lev Yashin makes his international debut (and keeps the first of many clean sheets) in a 7–0 win over Sweden. Read more about 'The Black Panther' on pages 19 and 34.

SEP 1955
The Soviet Union's biggest win – an 11–1 thumping of India.

DEC 1956
A 1–0 win over Yugoslavia secures Olympic gold medals all round.

JUL 1972
Oleh Blokhin makes a goalscoring international debut against Finland. Blokhin went on to become the most-capped Soviet player of all time with 112 caps, and top scorer with 42 goals.

JUN 1958
A first World Cup appearance ends in elimination at the hands of hosts Sweden in the quarter-finals.

DEC 1924
The Soviet Union wins its first-ever international, beating Turkey 3–0.

OCT 1897
The birth of Russian football, as the catchily named St Petersburg Circle of Lovers of Sport face Vasilievsky Island Football Society in the nation's first recorded match.

NOV 1973
Bizarre scenes in Chile, as the Soviets make a political stand and refuse to travel to the second leg of their World Cup qualifying play-off. Chile take to the field against no opposition, and are put through to the Finals. The Soviets would go on to miss out on qualification to the next World Cup and the next three Euros.

OCT 1958
A bad day in London, as England inflict a record 5–0 defeat.

HIGHS AND LOWS

JUN 1988
A classy Soviet side makes it all the way to the Euro 1988 final, losing 2–0 to the Netherlands and *that* Marco van Basten goal.

DEC 2010
Russia are named hosts of the 2018 World Cup.

JUN 1994
Oleg Salenko scores five in a 6–1 win over Cameroon at World Cup 1994, but Russia still go out at the group stage.

JUN 2008
An upturn in fortunes as the magic touch of coach Guus Hiddink sees Russia go all the way to the Euro 2008 semi-finals.

OCT 1988
Another Olympic gold triumph, this time beating Brazil 2–1 in the final.

NOV 1991
The Soviet Union's last-ever match ends in a 3–0 win over Cyprus, sealing qualification for Euro 1992.

JUN 1995
Russia's biggest international win: a 7–0 walloping of San Marino.

AUG 1992
The Russia national team play their first match, beating Mexico 2–0.

AUG 2002
Russia's most-capped player, Sergei Ignashevich, makes his international debut against Sweden.

JUN 2012
Russia exit Euro 2012 at the group stage – a feat which would be repeated at the 2014 World Cup and Euro 2016. Can they go further in 2018?

JUN 1992
Competing as the CIS, a poor performance sees them finish bottom of their Euro 1992 group, losing 3–0 to Scotland in their last game.

OCT 2005
Russia fail to qualify for the 2006 World Cup, not returning to the world stage until 2014.

RUSSIA'S FAVOURITE SON

▼ A typically full-stretch Yashin leaps to keep out a West German free-kick during the 1966 World Cup semi-final at Goodison Park.

RUSSIAN FOOTBALL'S TOP FIVE LEGENDS

5 Rinat Dasaev
In Russia, Dasaev is considered second only to Yashin when it comes to the question of best-ever keeper. Dasaev played 91 times for his country, including the Euro 1988 final.

4 Valentin Ivanov
This prolific striker holds the distinction of having finished joint-top scorer at both Euro 1960 and World Cup 1962.

3 Viktor Onopko
This stylish defender was Russia's Mr Dependable, playing 109 times for Russia plus four times for the CIS.

2 Oleh Blokhin
Blokhin holds two records for the Soviet Union: most appearances (112) and most goals scored (42). He also won a whole host of awards, including European Footballer of the Year in 1975.

1 Lev Yashin
To some he's 'The Black Panther', to others 'The Black Spider'. To us, and millions of Russians, he's simply 'The Legend'.

◀ In his trademark all-black, Yashin and teammates emerge from the tunnel for the 1966 semi-final.

Ask any Russian to tell you the greatest player to have represented their country, and one name will always come up: goalkeeper Lev Yashin.

Always dressed in an intimidating all-black kit, Yashin was renowned for his immense presence, quick reflexes, athleticism and near-psychic anticipation. But perhaps his greatest contribution to the game was the way in which he revolutionized his position, setting the standards for goalkeeping as we know it today.

In an age when keepers seemed permanently glued to their line, Yashin intercepted crosses, rushed out to challenge attackers, screamed commands at his defenders and was one of the first to throw the ball out instead of simply booting it clear. Way before Manuel Neuer became known as the

ultimate 'sweeper keeper', there was Lev Yashin: the trailblazer for goalies everywhere.

Yashin was the rock that the Soviet golden generation of the 1950s and 1960s was built upon. He played a pivotal role in helping them win Olympic gold in 1956, followed by the European Championship four years later.

At club level, Yashin stayed loyal to his beloved Dinamo Moscow. He played his entire 22-year career there, winning five league titles and three cups. Along the way, he kept an incredible 270 clean sheets, saved a reported 150 penalties and was a three-time winner of the USSR's Best Goalkeeper award.

His iconic black kit, coupled with his cat-like reactions, earned him the nickname 'The Black Panther'. He was also known as 'The Black Spider', again for his black kit, and

his ability to keep the ball out of his goal like a spider with eight legs.

After hanging up his gloves, he was awarded the respected Soviet title of Master of Sport, as well as the Order of Lenin – the highest civilian honour bestowed upon citizens of his country. But perhaps his finest personal accolade was winning the 1963 Ballon d'Or. To this day, he remains the first and only keeper to have won the prestigious award. Such is the impact Lev Yashin had on the game that FIFA even named an award after him (fittingly, the Lev Yashin Award is given to the best goalkeeper of each World Cup).

But the true test of Yashin's legend is that time has not diminished it. Even though many of today's fans have never seen him play, he remains regarded as simply the greatest goalkeeper ever.

PORTUGAL

With a team built around Real Madrid powerhouse Cristiano Ronaldo, Portugal head for Russia on the back of their triumphant performance at Euro 2016. Can they add the World Cup to their trophy cabinet and make it a double?

WORLD CUP NUMBERS

ATTENDED	6
GAMES PLAYED	26
WIN PERCENTAGE	50%
WORLD CUPS WON	0
MILES TO MOSCOW	2,438

MOST CAPS	147	MOST GOALS	79
CRISTIANO RONALDO		CRISTIANO RONALDO	

THEIR GREATEST MOMENT
═ EURO 2016 ═

After making it all the way through to the final against hosts France, disaster struck for Portugal when Ronaldo, their captain and spearhead, hobbled off early with a knee injury. Legend has it that at the half-time break, defender Pepe told his devastated teammates that they had to 'win it for Ronaldo' – and win it they did, with a 25-yard strike from forward Eder in extra-time. After many fruitless attempts, Portugal were finally the winners of one of football's major international trophies.

Position: Forward
Caps: 64 (1961–73)
Goals: 41
Clubs: Sporting Clube de Lourenço Marques, Benfica, Boston Minutemen, Monterrey, Toronto Metros-Croatia, Beira-Mar, Las Vegas Quicksilvers, União de Tomar, New Jersey Americans

THE LEGEND

EUSÉBIO

An incredible all-round athlete who was said to be able to run the 100 metres in just 11 seconds at the age of 16, Eusébio remains an icon of the Portuguese game. He was the Portuguese league's top scorer on seven occasions, European Golden Boot winner twice and the top scorer at the 1966 World Cup. Playing with precision and passion, the man known in his homeland as 'The King' was the blueprint for the modern striker.

★ THE RISING STAR ★

ANDRÉ SILVA

The youngest player to score a hat-trick for Portugal, 22-year-old André Silva has formed an impressive partnership with Cristiano Ronaldo. Opportunistic and composed in front of goal, the speedy Milan striker is a constant problem for defenders, scoring an impressive 9 goals in 10 games during his country's World Cup qualifying campaign.

DID YOU KNOW?

Portugal weren't invited to participate in the inaugural World Cup, and tried and failed to qualify for every tournament between 1934 and 1962. They finally qualified in 1966, finishing in third place. It would be another 20 years until their next World Cup appearance.

★ THE RISING STAR ★

FRANCISCO ROMÁN ALARCÓN SUÁREZ

ISCO

Francisco Román Alarcón Suárez is better known by one name – Isco. At Real Madrid they also call him *Magia*, simply meaning 'magic', and the midfield magician certainly displayed his sorcery when he performed the perfect nutmeg in Spain's qualifier against Italy, dribbling the ball straight through the legs of Paris Saint-Germain's Marco Verratti. Expect Isco to relish his first appearance at a World Cup.

DID YOU KNOW?

Between November 2006 and June 2009, Spain remained undefeated for 35 consecutive matches, a world record they share with Brazil. They're also currently undefeated in World Cup qualifying matches since 1993 – that's 62 games without a defeat.

 SPAIN

After disappointing performances at both the 2014 World Cup and Euro 2016, *La Roja* ('The Red') are looking to recapture the magic that saw them dominate the international scene between 2008 and 2012.

WORLD CUP NUMBERS

ATTENDED	14
GAMES PLAYED	59
WIN PERCENTAGE	49%
WORLD CUPS WON	1
MILES TO MOSCOW	▶ 2,140

MOST CAPS 167	MOST GOALS 59
IKER CASILLAS	**DAVID VILLA**

THEIR GREATEST MOMENT
= 2010 WORLD CUP =

Fresh from winning Euro 2008, Spain became football's eighth world champions in a bad-tempered final against the Netherlands in South Africa. In a match that saw the ref dish out 13 yellow cards and one red, they were saved from the trauma of penalties when Andrés Iniesta scored the game's only goal with four minutes left of extra-time. Two years later, Spain's golden generation completed their international hat-trick by also winning Euro 2012.

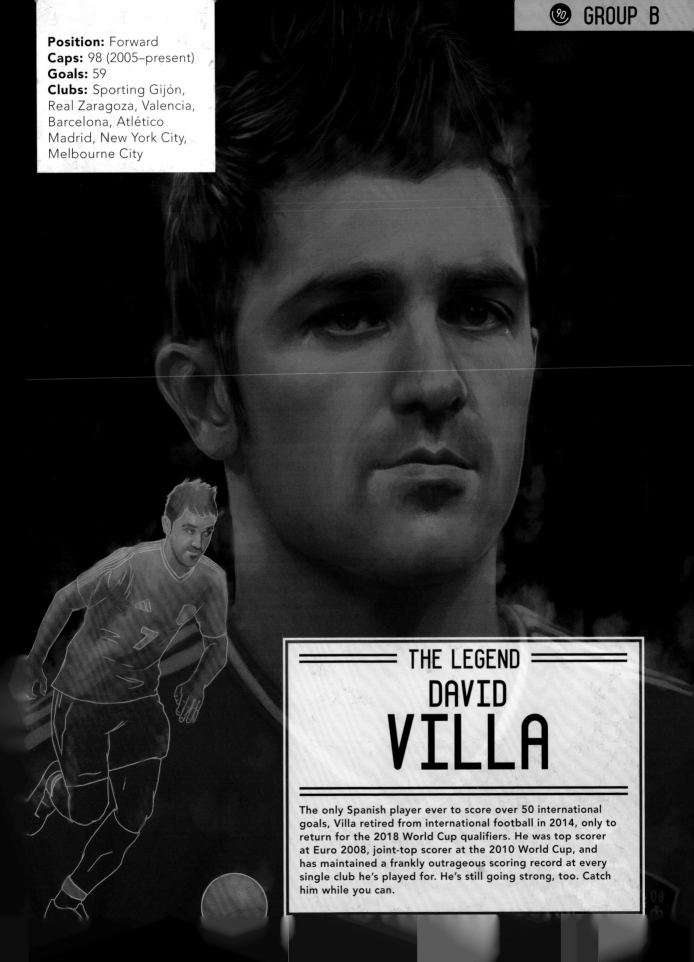

Position: Forward
Caps: 98 (2005–present)
Goals: 59
Clubs: Sporting Gijón, Real Zaragoza, Valencia, Barcelona, Atlético Madrid, New York City, Melbourne City

THE LEGEND
DAVID
VILLA

The only Spanish player ever to score over 50 international goals, Villa retired from international football in 2014, only to return for the 2018 World Cup qualifiers. He was top scorer at Euro 2008, joint-top scorer at the 2010 World Cup, and has maintained a frankly outrageous scoring record at every single club he's played for. He's still going strong, too. Catch him while you can.

MOROCCO

Returning to the World Cup after a 20-year absence, the Atlas Lions will hope to have better luck than they had at France 1998, when they crashed out at the group stage despite drawing with Norway and thrashing Scotland.

WORLD CUP NUMBERS

ATTENDED	4
GAMES PLAYED	13
WIN PERCENTAGE	15%
WORLD CUPS WON	0
MILES TO MOSCOW	2,750

MOST CAPS 115	MOST GOALS 42
NOUREDDINE NAYBET	AHMED FARAS

THEIR GREATEST MOMENT
═ 1986 WORLD CUP ═

Mexico 1986 was a ground-breaking World Cup for Morocco, and for African football. The Moroccans became the first African nation to top their group, finishing ahead of England, Poland and Portugal. In doing so, they also became the first African side to go through to the second round, where they met eventual runners-up West Germany. In a nail-biting clash, there were no goals until the 88th minute, when Lothar Matthäus struck home a devastating long-range free-kick to break Moroccan hearts.

Position: Forward
Caps: 77 (1965–79)
Goals: 42
Clubs: Chabab Mohammédia

THE LEGEND
AHMED
FARAS

Morocco's captain for eight consecutive years between 1971 and 1979, Ahmed Faras played in both the 1970 World Cup and the 1972 Olympics. Perhaps his finest moment in a Morocco shirt, though, was when he led his country to African Cup of Nations glory – for the only time in their history – in 1976. Faras remains Morocco's all-time leading goalscorer, and was also prolific for his hometown club, Chabab Mohammédia, to whom he remained loyal for his entire career.

THE RISING STAR ★

ACHRAF

HAKIMI

st 19 years of age, this versatile
nder looks destined to have a
uture ahead of him. Having
ressed through Real Madrid's
h system, he has already broken
the first team for the Spanish
s. He started Morocco's last
qualifying matches and scored
rst international goal in their
win over Mali, so has made a
g claim for a starting
e in Russia.

DID YOU KNOW?

Morocco's French-born manager,
Hervé Renard, is the only coach to
have won the African Cup of Nations
with two different countries: Zambia in
2012 and Ivory Coast in 2015. He also
had a spell in charge of Angola, making
Morocco the fourth African nation
he's managed. He's even
squeezed in a stint as
assistant manager
of Ghana.

★ THE RISING STAR ★

MILAD

MOHAMMADI

Russian fans will need no introduction to this lightning-quick left-back. After impressing with Rah Ahan in his native Iranian league, he secured a move to Russian Premier League side Akhmat Grozny in 2016. Since then he's become a regular fixture in Akhmat's line-up, and is considered one of Asian football's top talents.

DID YOU KNOW?

Iran's shirt for the 2014 World Cup featured an image of an Asiatic cheetah to raise awareness of the highly endangered species, which currently faces extinction.

IRAN

Team Melli ('The National Team') have a strong combo of seasoned pros and fresh young talent, and breezed through the Asian qualifiers without losing a single match. However, they've never progressed beyond the group stages in any of their four previous World Cup appearances. Could this be their year to change that?

WORLD CUP NUMBERS

ATTENDED	4
GAMES PLAYED	12
WIN PERCENTAGE	8%
WORLD CUPS WON	0
MILES TO MOSCOW	1,533

MOST CAPS 151	MOST GOALS ⚽ 109
JAVAD NEKOUNAM	ALI DAEI

THEIR GREATEST MOMENT

= 1998 WORLD CUP =

After narrowly defeating Australia on away goals in a tightly fought play-off, Iran progressed to France 1998 where the most-hyped game in their history awaited. Against the USA, their long-standing political enemies, Iran pulled off an unlikely 2–1 win – their only victory at a World Cup to this day. They failed to make it out of the group, but left France with their heads held high.

For more on that USA v. Iran match, head to page 131.

Position: Forward
Caps: 149 (1993–2006)
Goals: 109
Clubs: Esteghlal Ardabil, Taxirani, Bank Tejarat, Persepolis (twice), Al-Sadd, Arminia Bielefeld, Bayern Munich, Hertha BSC, Al Shabab, Saba Battery, Saipa

══ THE LEGEND ══
ALI
DAEI

Ali Daei has scored more international goals than any other male player in history, and is the only player to have scored over 100 times for his country. His playing career included Champions League appearances for both Bayern Munich and Hertha BSC (and a Bundesliga title win with the former) – but it's his goals in an Iran shirt for which he will always be known.

OUR RUSSIA

It's the biggest country in Europe, packed with music, art, culture, history, diversity and, of course, football. Here is our first-hand guide to the cities and stadiums that will make 2018 a World Cup to savour.

KALININGRAD

Kaliningrad is a Russian city like no other – primarily because it's not technically in Russia. This small coastal city is the capital of Kaliningrad Oblast, a Russian exclave located about 370 miles from the Russian mainland, between Poland and Lithuania. Thanks to its westerly location, World Cup visitors to Kaliningrad should get to enjoy warmer temperatures than those heading further east.

KALININGRAD STADIUM

Construction of the Kaliningrad Stadium (also known as the Arena Baltika) got off to a slow start due to its precarious position on an island in the middle of the city. In homage to the Baltic region where the city resides, the ground's exterior is blue and white. With a capacity of around 35,000, it's the tournament's smallest host venue.

▼ The city of Kaliningrad, with its new World Cup stadium popping up in the background.

MEET THE LOCALS

Baltika Kaliningrad's fixture against league rivals Luch-Energia Vladivostok is the longest away trip in domestic football. The journey from one to the other is nearly 13,000 miles – almost a quarter of the way around the globe.

COOL FOR CATS

Visit the city's King's Gate and you'll be greeted by the Prussian Cat: a bronze feline statue said to bring wealth and luck to all who give it a scratch behind the ear.

KAZAN

Kazan is a fabulous melting-pot of ethnicities where the large Muslim and Orthodox Christian populations live alongside the ethnic Tatar community, who founded the city over 1,000 years ago. With the city's renowned passion for sport, its massive student population and the Tatar people's famous love of food, Kazan is in many ways the perfect World Cup host city.

KAZAN ARENA

Designed by the same firm as Wembley Stadium and the Emirates, the Kazan Arena didn't come cheap, but it's certainly ambitious. Its swooping aluminium roof was apparently designed to represent a 'water-borne flowering plant'.

MEET THE LOCALS

Rubin Kazan take their name from the Russian word for 'ruby' – hence their ruby-red kits.

GOING UNDERGROUND

Kazan's Metro is officially the shortest in the world. To get from one end to the other takes just ten minutes.

MOSCOW

The biggest city in not only Russia but the whole of Europe, Moscow is universally recognized as one of the most influential cultural hubs in the world. This incredible location boasts endless sights, whether you're outside discovering Red Square's magnificent Saint Basil's Cathedral and 900-year-old Kremlin, underground among the breath-taking art covering the Metro's platforms, or indoors at the numerous art galleries.

▲ The Spartak Stadium: red, white and very easy to spot.

LUZHNIKI STADIUM

With a capacity of around 81,000 and a history of hosting major world sporting events, it's fitting that the Luzhniki has been chosen to host the tournament's opening match and final. Constructed in 1956 to resemble the Colosseum in Rome, its World Cup re-build has left the 1950s exterior undisturbed while radically modernizing the interior.

SPARTAK STADIUM

Home to Spartak Moscow, arguably Russia's most popular club, the 43,000-seat Spartak Stadium (also known as the Otkritie Arena) will host five matches. Its striking red-and-white shell makes it an unmissable landmark.

MEET THE LOCALS

Moscow boasts a number of famous Russian club sides within its boundaries: Spartak, CSKA, Lokomotiv, Dinamo and Torpedo. A new club, Ararat Moscow, was founded just last year to represent the city's Armenian community, and quickly signed up ex-Spurs striker Roman Pavlyuchenko.

MONEY MONEY MONEY

Moscow has the highest concentration of billionaires in the world – including Chelsea owner Roman Abramovich (when he's not in London).

NIZHNY NOVGOROD

A relaxing former merchant city that sits at the crossing of two rivers, Nizhny Novgorod is using its host status to do some fine-tuning. Despite already being considered one of European Russia's most picturesque places, the local government has spent almost $100 million refurbishing its airport, expanding its rail network and, of course, building its new stadium.

NIZHNY NOVGOROD STADIUM

Plans for this brand-new 45,000-seat venue include a blue-and-white windproof membrane, encircled by triangular columns.

MEET THE LOCALS

Olimpiets Nizhny Novgorod are one of the new kids of Russian football – they were founded in 2015, and play in the country's third tier.

BABUSHKA-ЧА-ЧА!

Nizhny Novgorod is the home of the world-famous babushka doll (otherwise known as a matryoshka) – an ornamental doll containing another doll (and another doll, and another doll . . .).

▲ Your go-to souvenir for any trip to this neck of the woods.

ROSTOV-ON-DON

The largest city in southern Russia, everything about Rostov-on-Don revolves around its river. The Don River gave the city its name, access to goods in its early years and a large embankment that becomes the life of the city every summer.

MEET THE LOCALS

FC Rostov were dubbed 'the Russian Leicester' during their unlikely challenge for the 2015/16 title. They ultimately came second, but reached the Champions League, where they defeated Bayern Munich at home in the group stage.

ALL THAT JAZZ

Different types of music play a big part in Rostov culture, and jazz is the most important of the lot. The city plays host to a number of international jazz festivals and even has its own jazz school.

ROSTOV ARENA

Constructed on the previously undeveloped southern bank of the Don River, the Rostov Arena will have a legacy long after the World Cup. The city's mayor hailed the stadium as a catalyst for 'developing a new and exciting part of the city' and, post-tournament, the 45,000-capacity ground will become the home of the city's beloved FC Rostov.

▲ The brand-new Rostov Arena, host to five matches at the 2018 World Cup.

SAMARA

Samara is a point of pride for Russians thanks to the role it played in the country's pioneering space programme. Samara's factories produce the Soyuz rocket, which is used in 70 per cent of the world's space flights to this day. Visitors are reminded of this everywhere they look, from the city's statues to its museums and, now, its brand-new Samara Arena – which is also known as the Cosmos Arena.

SAMARA ARENA

Like everything else in the city, the Samara Arena has been inspired by the aeronautical world, and takes the shape of a domed space object. The dome required over 2,500 workers and spans 330 metres. Made up of 32 panels, each weighing 134 tonnes, the 44,000-seater is destined to be a new iconic landmark for the city.

MEET THE LOCALS

Krylia Sovetov Samara have had some notable players in their time, including Andrei Kanchelskis and Jan Koller.

INFINITY AND BEYOND

The Vostok, the spacecraft used in the first-ever manned spaceflight, was built right here in Samara. It safely transported Yuri Gagarin into the cosmos in 1961.

◄ Is it a bird? Is it a plane? Nope, it's the impressive spacecraft entrance to Samara's Space Museum.

SARANSK

Located at the basin of the Volga River, Saransk is the smallest host city of the tournament. As the capital of the Republic of Mordovia, Saransk is home to a Mordvin community, an ethnic minority known for their folk art.

MORDOVIA ARENA

This bowl-shaped arena has been built in the shape and colour of the sun, a significant symbol in Mordovian culture.

MEET THE LOCALS

Mordovia Saransk will move into the Mordovia Arena after the tournament – with the capacity being cut down from 44,000 to around 28,000.

WALK THIS WAY

This won't be the first time Saransk has been a World Cup host. Six years ago, its streets were turned into the tracks for the 2012 World Race Walking Cup.

▲ The 2012 World Cup (for race walking).

SOCHI

With its sub-tropical climate, abundance of *banyas* (a traditional Russian steam bath) and position on the 'Russian Riviera', Sochi is a host city with plenty to offer besides football. Still, there's a big love of sport in this place. With a giant sports museum in the centre of town and the 2014 Winter Olympics under its belt, Sochi is primed and ready for World Cup duty.

FISHT STADIUM

Originally built for the Winter Olympics, the Fisht Stadium has had some renovations made for the World Cup, with the roof coming off and additional stands going up at either end. Its all-white exterior is intended to resemble the crest and colour of the nearby Mount Fisht.

MEET THE LOCALS

Sochi has had a difficult time of it when it comes to club-level football. With Zhemchuzhina-Sochi and Sochi-04 both having been dissolved, lower-league outfit FC Sochi are now the city's main hope.

SUN, SEA AND SOCHI

Sochi is a major tourist destination, attracting two million visitors annually (which is almost five times its population).

▼ The Fisht Stadium is used to major events, having hosted both the opening and closing ceremonies of the 2014 Winter Olympics.

SAINT PETERSBURG

Spread across a series of islands next to the Neva River delta, Saint Petersburg is Russia's second city. It's considered a cultural heartland thanks to an imperial past that left a legacy of art and architecture for future generations to enjoy. Walking its cobblestoned streets, admiring its gold-rimmed cathedrals and venturing into its numerous theatres, ballet schools and art museums, you'll instantly understand why it's listed as a UNESCO World Heritage Site.

HIDDEN GOLD

The main dome of St Isaac's Cathedral is covered with 100 kg of pure gold. During the Second World War, it was sneakily coated with grey paint to hide it from passing enemy aircraft.

SAINT PETERSBURG STADIUM

Dominating the city's skyline, the imposing Saint Petersburg Stadium (also known as the Krestovsky Stadium or Zenit Arena) is the pinnacle of technical design, featuring a sliding roof and a retractable pitch. With a capacity of 68,000, the brand-new arena is the second-biggest venue of the tournament and will host seven matches including a semi-final and the third-place play-off.

MEET THE LOCALS

The 'zenit' part of Zenit Saint Petersburg means 'zenith' – a name once commonly used by Russian teams representing military industrial plants and factories. The club is no longer affiliated to the Leningrad Metalworks Plant (LMZ), but the name stuck.

▲ The Church of the Saviour on Spilled Blood, one of Saint Petersburg's most striking sights.

▶ *The Motherland Calls* statue makes quite a statement. And that statement is 'I. Am. Massive.'

VOLGOGRAD

Volgograd is a Russian city with a story to tell. In its 500-year existence, it's been the centre of many a conflict, including the Battle of Stalingrad (the city's former name), universally recognized as having changed the course of the Second World War. After the war the city was rebuilt from scratch, as can be seen from the magnificent 1950s and 1960s Soviet architecture dotting the landscape.

MONUMENTAL

If you like gigantic statues, Volgograd is the place for you. At 87 metres, the sword-brandishing *The Motherland Calls* is the tallest statue in Europe, and the tallest statue of a woman anywhere in the world. The city is also home to a huge statue of Vladimir Lenin.

VOLGOGRAD ARENA

Residing upon the banks of the Volga River and only a short distance from *The Motherland Calls*, the newly built Volgograd Arena is situated on prime real estate. To keep the stadium as sustainable as possible, it's being built exclusively with eco-friendly materials and will include a water recycling system.

MEET THE LOCALS

Rotor Volgograd were originally called Traktor, after the Stalingrad Tractor Factory. Later in their history, they were owned by a factory that made car parts, hence 'Rotor' (the rotating part of a car's motor).

▲ The Yekaterinburg Arena: new on the inside, historic and imposing on the outside.

YEKATERINBURG

Nestled among the striking Ural Mountains, Yekaterinburg is the most easterly host city. Sitting on the frontier of European and Asian Russia, the city is influenced by both continents. Visitors will find themselves immersed in a diverse culture that appreciates good food, humour and lots of street art.

YEKATERINBURG ARENA

A truly unique construction, the Yekaterinburg Arena is a fantastic combination of old and new. With the site of the stadium steeped in over 100 years of sporting history (a velodrome was first built on this location in 1900, then replaced by a stadium in the 1950s), designers decided to incorporate its legacy into the new venue. So, while a roof has been added and the interior built from scratch, the Soviet-era exterior has been preserved.

MEET THE LOCALS

Ural Sverdlovsk Oblast have been a bit of a yo-yo club over the years, but they currently enjoy a place in the country's top flight. Like many Russian clubs, they have proud industrial roots and started out as a factory side.

SHOW ME THE FUNNY

Yekaterinburg is known for producing many comedians and is the birthplace of *Ural Dumplings*, one of Russia's most popular TV comedy hits.

FRANCE

Write off *Les Bleus* ('The Blues') at your peril. While their dream-team era of 1998–2000 is now a distant memory, they travel to Russia as a major force and boast a young, exciting team.

WORLD CUP NUMBERS

ATTENDED	14
GAMES PLAYED	59
WIN PERCENTAGE	47%
WORLD CUPS WON	★ 1
MILES TO MOSCOW	▶ 1,547

MOST CAPS  142	MOST GOALS 51
LILIAN THURAM	THIERRY HENRY

THEIR GREATEST MOMENT
= 1998 WORLD CUP =

France may have gone into the 1998 World Cup as hosts, but Brazil were the hot favourites. *Les Bleus* hadn't even qualified for the previous World Cup – and yet, on home soil and boasting a squad at the peak of its powers, they were unstoppable. In the most one-sided World Cup final for 28 years, Zidane scored twice and Emmanuel Petit added a killer third to complete a rampant 3–0 win.

Position: Midfielder
Caps: 108 (1994–2006)
Goals: 31
Clubs: Cannes, Bordeaux, Juventus, Real Madrid

THE LEGEND
ZINEDINE
ZIDANE

Zizou has come a long way since his days of learning his trade on the streets of Marseille. Surely the greatest French footballer of all time, his glittering playing career included one World Cup win, one European Championship win, two Italian titles, one Spanish title, one Champions League, one Ballon d'Or and three World Player of the Year awards. As a manager, his success shows no signs of slowing down, and he's already lifted a further two Champions League trophies with Real Madrid.

★ THE RISING STAR ★

KYLIAN

MBAPPÉ

This 19-year-old striker broke many of the legendary Thierry Henry's records while at Monaco. At 16, he became the youngest player to make the Monaco first team (a record Henry had held for 21 years) and two months later he wiped out another of Henry's achievements by becoming the club's youngest-ever scorer. Having already broken into the national side and made a move to Paris Saint-Germain, Mbappé looks destined to have a massive future.

DID YOU KNOW?

A group of French football administrators, led by Jules Rimet, is credited with coming up with the idea for the first World Cup in 1930. Rimet was President of FIFA for over 30 years, and the original trophy used for the World Cup was named after him.

THE RISING STAR ★

JACKSON
IRVINE

After moving halfway around the world to Scotland to sign for Celtic, Irvine had spells with Kilmarnock, Ross County and Burton Albion before clinching a move to Hull City. Despite playing for Scotland at U19 level (qualifying through his Scottish father), he committed his future to Australia and featured throughout their World Cup qualifying campaign. Look out for the long-haired midfielder's driving runs and habit of shooting from distance.

DID YOU KNOW?

Australia is the only nation to have been champion of two separate confederations. The Socceroos won the OFC Nations Cup four times between 1980 and 2004, and then lifted the AFC Asian Cup in 2015. They made the switch from Oceania to the Asian Football Confederation in 2005.

AUSTRALIA

After a disappointing early exit from the 2014 World Cup, Australia bounced back to win the 2015 AFC Asian Cup on home soil. With a clutch of younger players now in the gold and green, can the Socceroos finally progress past the round of 16?

WORLD CUP NUMBERS

ATTENDED	4
GAMES PLAYED	13
WIN PERCENTAGE	15%
WORLD CUPS WON	0
MILES TO MOSCOW	9,018

MOST CAPS 109	MOST GOALS 50
MARK SCHWARZER	TIM CAHILL

THEIR GREATEST MOMENT
= 2006 WORLD CUP =

Germany 2006 was Australia's first World Cup appearance since 1974, and it turned out to be their best. After finishing second in a tough group that also included Brazil, Croatia and Japan, the Aussies produced a brave display against Italy in the round of 16. But it wasn't to be: five minutes into stoppage time, Francesco Totti slotted home a last-gasp penalty to send the Italians through. To this day, it means Australia are the only country ever to have been knocked out of the World Cup by the last kick of a match.

Position: Forward/Midfielder
Caps: 104 (2002–present)
Goals: 50
Clubs: Millwall, Everton, New York Red Bulls, Shanghai Shenhua, Hangzhou Greentown, Melbourne City

THE LEGEND
TIM CAHILL

Born in Sydney to an English father and Samoan mother, Cahill moved to England in the late 1990s to sign for Millwall. However, he's perhaps best known for his time at Everton, where he made 226 appearances and scored 56 goals, many of which came from his head. He's one of an elite group of players who have scored at three separate World Cups (2006, 2010 and 2014), and he's not done yet: he scored twice against Syria in the play-off win that helped to seal Australia's place in Russia.

PERU

Back at the World Cup for the first time since 1982, Peru knocked New Zealand out of the qualifying play-offs to become the final country to qualify for Russia.

WORLD CUP NUMBERS

ATTENDED	4
GAMES PLAYED	15
WIN PERCENTAGE	27%
WORLD CUPS WON	0
MILES TO MOSCOW	7,866

MOST CAPS 128	MOST GOALS 32
ROBERTO PALACIOS	PAOLO GUERRERO

THEIR GREATEST MOMENT

== 1970 WORLD CUP ==

1970 saw Peru's first World Cup appearance since 1930, and was a tonic for a country reeling from a devastating earthquake that killed over 70,000 Peruvians just days before the competition started. Determined to raise their nation's spirits, Peru played with obvious and infectious joy, and made it all the way to the quarter-finals and a date with the mighty Brazil. In the end they lost 4–2, but made a lasting impression on the watching world with both their skill and resilience in the face of such tragedy.

Position: Midfielder
Caps: 81 (1968–82)
Goals: 26
Club: Alianza Lima (four times), Basel, Porto, Fort Lauderdale Strikers (twice), South Florida Sun, Miami Sharks

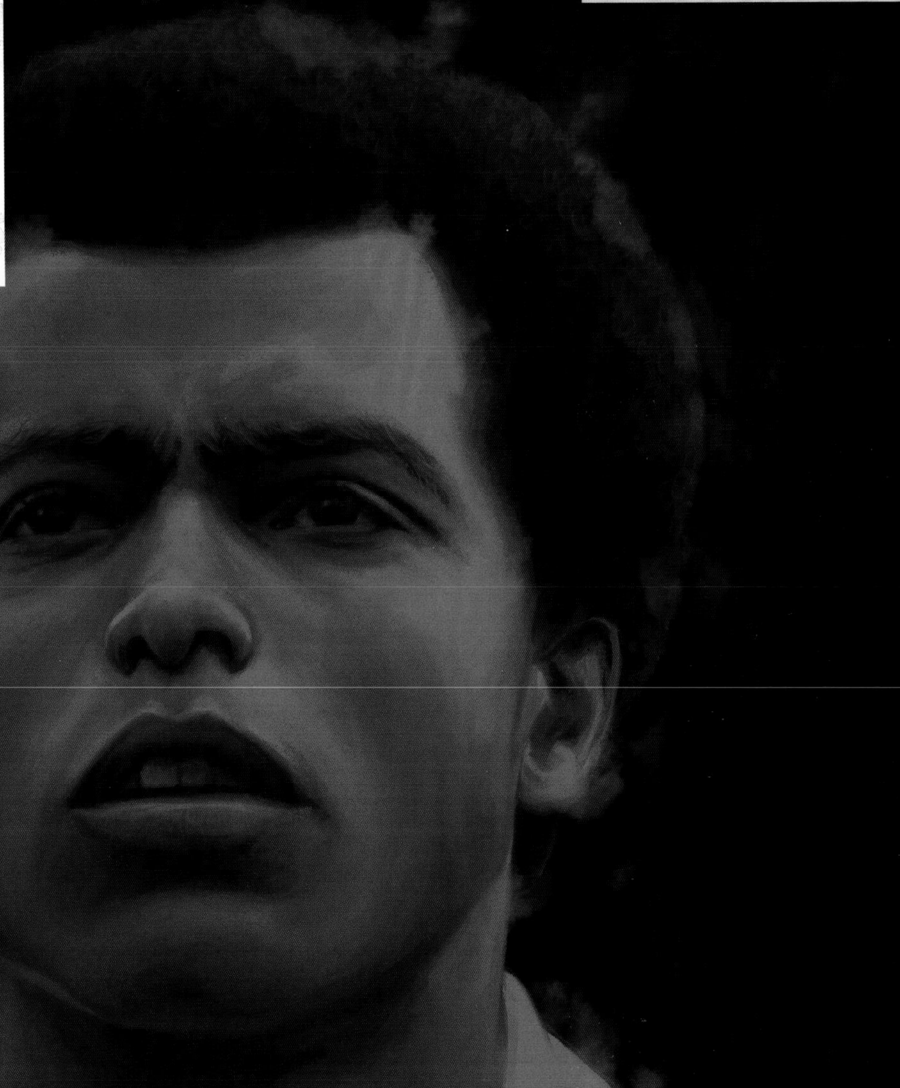

THE LEGEND
TEÓFILO CUBILLAS

Name-checked by Pelé as one of the world's greats, Cubillas was the sort of player you'd never tire of watching. Nicknamed *El Nene* ('The Babe'), he was the beating heart of Peru's midfield for 14 years, and was awarded young player of the tournament at Mexico 1970. Today, he remains one of only three players to have scored five or more goals at two separate World Cups (alongside Miroslav Klose and Thomas Müller) and consistently appears in lists of the finest players to have graced the game.

★ THE RISING STAR ★

RENATO

TAPIA

At 22, this versatile defensive midfielder is regarded as one of his country's brightest emerging talents. After a spell with FC Twente, he moved across the Netherlands to Feyenoord and picked up a 2016/17 league winners' medal. Back home in Peru, he's established himself as a regular for his national team and started both legs of his country's play-off victory against New Zealand.

DID YOU KNOW?

With the scores level after Peru and Brazil's two-legged semi-final of the 1975 Copa América, the winner was decided not on penalties, but by the drawing of lots. Peru won the draw, and went on to win the whole tournament.

★ THE RISING STAR ★

ANDREAS

CHRISTENSEN

Having emerged through the youth system of Danish side Brøndby, this talented defender secured a dream move to Chelsea on a free transfer in 2013. After an impressive loan spell with Borussia Mönchengladbach in Germany, he returned to England to break into Chelsea's first team. Now aged 22, he's also become a regular for Denmark, and scored his first international goal in the World Cup qualifying play-off win over Ireland.

DID YOU KNOW?

Denmark's fans are known as the Roligans, thanks to their stance against hooliganism. The word comes from the Danish term *rolig*, meaning 'peace and calm'.

DENMARK

Other than a run to the quarter-finals in 1998, Denmark have struggled to make an impact at the World Cup, often failing to qualify. However, after hammering the Republic of Ireland 5–1 in the qualification play-offs, they'll head to Russia with fresh confidence.

WORLD CUP NUMBERS

ATTENDED	4
GAMES PLAYED	16
WIN PERCENTAGE	50%
WORLD CUPS WON	0
MILES TO MOSCOW	971

MOST CAPS 🧢 129	MOST GOALS ⚽ 52
PETER SCHMEICHEL	POUL NIELSEN & JON DAHL TOMASSON

THEIR GREATEST MOMENT
EURO 1992

Denmark's players expected to be on their holidays in the summer of 1992, but instead they ended up on a football pitch in Sweden, winning Europe's biggest international football tournament. When Yugoslavia were disqualified due to the outbreak of civil war, the Danes were called upon to take their place with less than two weeks to go until kick-off. In one of football's biggest fairy-tale stories, Richard Møller-Nielsen's side went all the way to the final, where they defied the odds to beat Germany 2–0 and lift the trophy.

Position: Goalkeeper
Caps: 129 (1987–2001)
Goals: 1
Clubs: Gladsaxe-Hero, Hvidovre, Brøndby, Manchester United, Sporting Lisbon, Aston Villa, Manchester City

THE LEGEND
PETER
SCHMEICHEL

A relative unknown when Sir Alex Ferguson brought him to Manchester United in 1991, Peter Schmeichel soon became a huge figure at Old Trafford with his blond hair, green jersey and habit of shrieking instructions at his often-terrified defenders. The fearless goalkeeper lifted ten trophies in his eight years at United, and also won Euro 1992 with his national team. When he wasn't pulling off spectacular, acrobatic saves, the Great Dane could occasionally be seen at the other end of the pitch, and scored an impressive 11 goals in his career. The Schmeichel name lives on in Danish football through his son, Kasper, who will be Denmark's number one in Russia.

QUALIFIER STORIES

Beginning three years before a ball is even kicked at the Finals, the World Cup's qualifying rounds create some of football's most emotional, exhilarating and unbelievable moments. Involving more than 200 nations competing in over 800 matches, they capture the attention of fans across the planet, from Chile to China. Here are some of the stand-out stories to have come out of the qualifiers.

THE QUALIFIER THAT STOPPED A WAR
SUDAN v. IVORY COAST

In October 2005, the national team of Ivory Coast headed to Sudan for a crucial World Cup qualifier.

Victory would mean the country qualified for the Finals for the first time in their nation's history. However, that was the last thing on the players' minds. Back home, their nation was in the midst of civil war, split by an ethnic and regional divide that had left thousands dead, and an upcoming national election threatened further bloodshed. Putting aside the situation back home for 90 minutes, the team won 3–1 and headed straight for the changing rooms where they celebrated wildly. Seeing an opportunity, captain Cyrille Domoraud invited

the media inside, grabbed a microphone and handed it to rising star and national hero Didier Drogba.

Drogba found the nearest camera, stared down the lens and pleaded:

'Men and women of Ivory Coast, from the north, south, centre, and west. We proved today that all Ivorians can co-exist and play together with a shared aim, to qualify for the World Cup. We promised you that the celebration would unite the people. Today, we beg you, on our knees . . . Pardonnez! [Forgive!] Pardonnez! Pardonnez!'

As he spoke, Drogba and his teammates knelt in unison on the

dressing-room floor, arms wrapped around each other's shoulders, with free hands lifted to their heads.

'The one country in Africa with so many riches must not descend into war. Please lay down your weapons. Hold elections. All will be better.'

Then Drogba and his teammates stood, smiled and began to sing: 'We want to have fun, so stop firing your guuuuuns! We want to have fun, so stop firing your guuuuuns!'

The election went by without violence and, by the time *Les Elephants*, as the national team are known, lined up for their first match at the 2006 World Cup, the civil war had ended. For many, the actions of the players proved to be the turning-point.

▶ 'In 2005, your efforts will be rewarded,' says the poster – and for Didier Drogba, they certainly were.

FACT FILE

SUDAN   **1**
IVORY COAST   **3**

8 October 2005, Al-Merrikh Stadium, Omdurman (Sudan)

AFRICAN QUALIFICATION
ROUND 2, GROUP 3

Ivory Coast went on to play at the 2006 World Cup, where they finished third in a tough group that also included Argentina, the Netherlands and Serbia & Montenegro.

▶ Despite a late goal from the heroic Drogba, Ivory Coast lost 2–1 to Argentina in their opening match of the 2006 World Cup in Germany. Back home in Abidjan, these fans came together to watch their nation's first-ever World Cup match.

THE QUALIFIER THAT STARTED A WAR

HONDURAS v. EL SALVADOR

By 1969, these two neighbouring Central American nations already had a rocky relationship. Thousands of Salvadoran migrant workers had been kicked out of Honduras, and the atmosphere between the two countries was one of extreme tension. So, when they were pitted against each other in a 'best of three' World Cup qualification series, all hell broke loose.

On the eve of the first match in Honduras, noisy locals kept El Salvador's players up all night with chanting and drumming. The next day, Honduras beat their exhausted opponents 1–0 with a goal in the last minute.

FACT FILE

HONDURAS	1
EL SALVADOR	0

8 June 1969, National Stadium, Tegucigalpa (Honduras)

EL SALVADOR	3
HONDURAS	0

15 June 1969, Flor Blanca National Stadium, San Salvador (El Salvador)

EL SALVADOR	3
HONDURAS	2
(AET)	

26 June 1969, Azteca Stadium, Mexico City (Mexico)

CONCACAF SEMI-FINAL ROUND, GROUP 2

El Salvador went on to defeat Haiti in the final round and progress to the 1970 World Cup, where they came bottom of a group containing the Soviet Union, Mexico and Belgium.

Immediately after the match, an 18-year-old Salvadoran girl called Amelia Bolaños tragically shot herself in the heart. El Salvador's press claimed she did it because she couldn't bear to see her nation defeated, and she was given a televised state funeral with the president, ministers and national team marching behind her flag-draped coffin.

In the aftermath, the next match saw the animosity taken to another level. When the Honduran players arrived at their hotel, it wasn't just noise they faced, but broken windows, rotten eggs and even dead rats. As the team made their way to the stadium (in armoured cars!), local mobs lined the streets holding portraits of 'national heroine' Bolaños. Honduran fans weren't lucky enough to have the same level of protection, and many were assaulted – two fatally – on their way to the match.

Pre-match, the Honduran flag was burned in front of the ferocious crowd and then replaced by a tattered dishrag. Unsurprisingly, Honduras lost the game 3–0, which was perhaps for the best. Their coach would later state that, had they won, they might not have got out alive.

With both nations having won one game, the third match on neutral territory in Mexico City would decide the winner. On the day of the match, El Salvador's coach and entire squad were called to the president's home, where they were told in no uncertain terms that it was their duty to defend their country's national honour.

In a packed stadium where more than 5,000 Mexican police kept the thousands of travelling fans apart, El Salvador triumphed 3–2 in extra-time.

In the aftermath, diplomatic relations between the two nations were officially severed, and war became inevitable. Less than three weeks later, the Salvadoran military launched a first attack on the Honduran capital, to which the Honduran air force then retaliated with air strikes. A ceasefire was called after less than a week, but by that point the infamous 'Football War' had taken over 2,000 lives on both sides.

▲ A historic display of friendship, as Honduras captain Ramón Maradiaga and his El Salvador rival Norberto Huezo shake hands before their World Cup qualifier in 1981.

THE FOOTBALL WAR: FAST-FORWARD

In the years following the notorious 'Football War', relations between El Salvador and Honduras gradually settled. Since then, the two countries have met many more times on the pitch.

In 1981, both made it into the region's final six-team World Cup qualifying group, knowing that only the top two would make it to Spain 1982. Going into the final round of matches, El Salvador needed Honduras – who had already qualified – to get at least a point against firm favourites Mexico. The Hondurans went on to secure a 0–0 draw in Tegucigalpa, and both nations qualified for the following summer's World Cup. Remarkably, the Honduras squad were then invited to El Salvador for dual celebrations. Changed times indeed.

Unfortunately, when the two sides reached Spain it wasn't to be. Both finished bottom of their groups, with the Salvadorans on the wrong end of a particularly painful 10–1 thumping from Hungary – which remains a record defeat at a World Cup to this day.

To read about more of the World Cup's biggest grudge matches, turn to page 128.

THE PHOTOS THAT QUALIFIED A NATION

🇧🇷 BRAZIL v. CHILE 🇨🇱

The situation here was simple. Chile had to win to qualify. Brazil had to win or draw. One hundred and sixty thousand packed into the Maracanã for one of the most hotly anticipated matches in South American qualifying history.

An hour into the match Brazil were 1–0 up and well on top of the game, and Chile's hopes seemed all but gone. But, as the hosts broke into the Chilean half again, a flare was thrown from the Brazilian stands. Down went Chilean goalkeeper Roberto Rojas, clutching his head in agonizing pain as blood poured from his forehead.

▼ Roberto Rojas goes down.

Rojas's teammates gestured furiously towards the Brazilian fans, inflaming the situation and prompting the referee to abandon the match before a riot broke out. For Brazil, the situation looked bleak. With no TV or mobile-phone footage to go on, it seemed certain that they'd be held accountable. If Chile were awarded the points, Brazil would drop to second in the group and miss out on World Cup qualification for the first time in their history.

However, there's a twist in the tale – and it's a pretty big one. Paulo Teixeira, a Brazilian pitch-side photographer, was adamant he had seen the flare land a metre or so away from Rojas. Unfortunately for him, he had failed to get a shot of the incident, and was struggling to find anyone who did . . . until he bumped into his good friend and fellow photographer, Ricardo Alfieri.

This being 1989, before the days of digital photography, an anxious wait ensued. Alfieri's shots were all on film and had to be developed. And, to make matters worse, Alfieri was working for a Japanese magazine and was on orders to send his undeveloped film directly to Tokyo.

In the meantime, Teixeira took matters into his own hands and told a local radio station what he had seen. Before he knew it, the head of the CBF (Brazil's FA) was in the room demanding to see the shots. And so it was that, late on a Sunday night, a photo lab was found and a developer pulled out of bed as two nations waited anxiously for the photos to develop.

Four hours later, the results were indisputable. Four clear shots showed the flare flying through the air before landing a metre from Rojas. The Chilean keeper would later admit that the blood came from a razor blade he had hidden in his glove before the match.

Punishment for the Chileans was severe. Not only did they lose their chance of making it to World Cup 1990, but they were also suspended from taking part in World Cup 1994. Rojas himself was given a lifetime ban from playing the game, while Chile's coach and team doctor were also hit with bans. Brazil, meanwhile, were awarded a 2–0 victory and secured their place in the draw for football's showpiece event.

FACT FILE

BRAZIL	2
CHILE	0

3 September 1989, Maracanã Stadium, Rio de Janeiro (Brazil)

SOUTH AMERICAN QUALIFICATION, GROUP 3

Brazil topped their three-team section and went on to top their group at Italy 1990, before going out to Argentina in the round of 16.

▶ Cláudio Taffarel, who played 101 times for Brazil and appeared in three World Cups.

▼ Careca, Brazil's goal machine who scored 30 goals in 64 matches from 1982 until 1993.

BRAZIL:
THE CLASS OF 1990

Had Brazil missed out on Italy 1990, here are just a few of the stars who would have had to make do with watching it on TV . . .

TAFFAREL Brazil's most-capped-ever goalkeeper, who – like many of the Class of 1990 – went on to lift the World Cup in 1994.

JORGINHO Supremely talented attacking right-back who terrorized opposition full-backs during a medal-packed decade that saw him win the World Cup, the Bundesliga and Japan's J.League.

BRANCO Don't let his famously disastrous 1996 stint at Middlesbrough fool you. On his day, this guy was one of the greatest left-backs of his generation, playing a total of 72 times for Brazil over 10 years.

DUNGA The midfield muscle of 1990s-era Brazil, Dunga also played at the 1994 and 1998 World Cups, and later returned to lead the team as manager at the World Cup in 2010.

CARECA Not only a legend for Brazil, but also for Napoli, where he lined up alongside Diego Maradona in surely one of football's ultimate dream teams.

ROMÁRIO Only Pelé and Ronaldo have scored more Brazil goals than this legendary striker. Injury restricted his Italy 1990 appearance to just 66 minutes – but he went on to win the Golden Ball player of the tournament award at USA 1994.

BEBETO World Cup, Copa América, Confederations Cup – Bebeto won them all. But he's perhaps best known for his rock-the-baby goal celebration at USA 1994. Oh, and he also scored an incredible 86 goals in 131 matches for Deportivo La Coruña.

ARGENTINA

They have been at every World Cup since 1974, but Argentina's place in Russia hung in the balance until a Lionel Messi hat-trick in their final qualification match saw them through. *La Albiceleste* ('The White and Blue Sky') will be pinning their hopes on more Messi magic over the summer.

WORLD CUP NUMBERS

ATTENDED	16
GAMES PLAYED	77
WIN PERCENTAGE	55%
WORLD CUPS WON	★ ★ 2
MILES TO MOSCOW	▶ 8,383

MOST CAPS	143
JAVIER ZANETTI	

MOST GOALS	⚽ 61
LIONEL MESSI	

THEIR GREATEST MOMENT

= 1986 WORLD CUP =

They'd already won the World Cup on their own turf in 1978, but Argentina's second triumph in Mexico eight years later was extra-special. Manager Carlos Bilardo's decision to give Maradona the captain's armband was not initially a popular one, but no one was complaining when he led the side all the way to a 3–2 win over West Germany in the final. There's no such thing as a one-man team, but the Diego-inspired Argentina side of 1986 comes about as close as you can get.

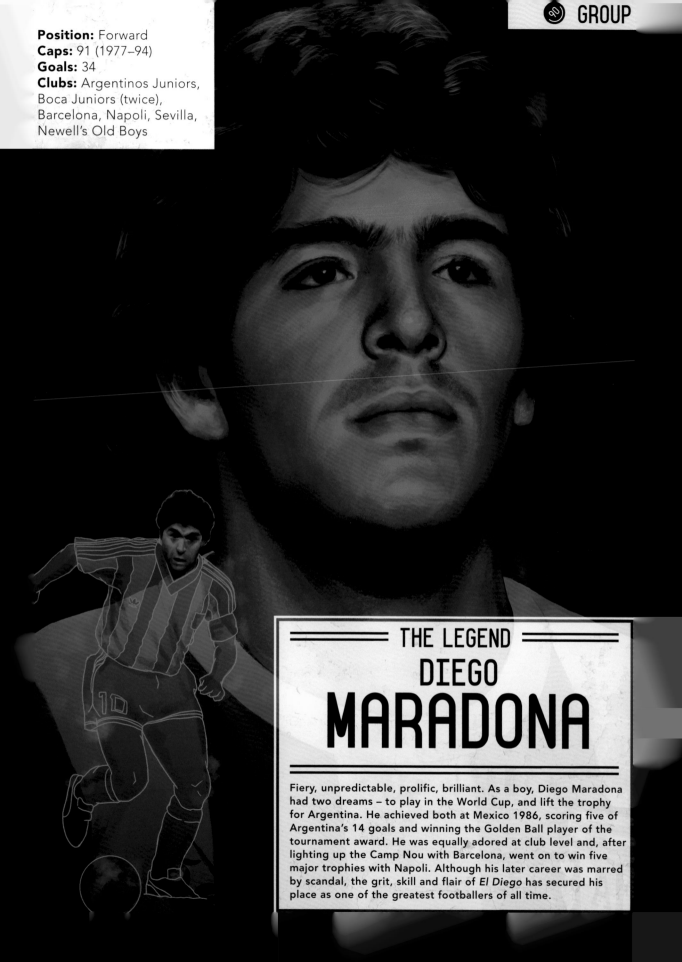

Position: Forward
Caps: 91 (1977–94)
Goals: 34
Clubs: Argentinos Juniors, Boca Juniors (twice), Barcelona, Napoli, Sevilla, Newell's Old Boys

THE LEGEND
DIEGO
MARADONA

Fiery, unpredictable, prolific, brilliant. As a boy, Diego Maradona had two dreams – to play in the World Cup, and lift the trophy for Argentina. He achieved both at Mexico 1986, scoring five of Argentina's 14 goals and winning the Golden Ball player of the tournament award. He was equally adored at club level and, after lighting up the Camp Nou with Barcelona, went on to win five major trophies with Napoli. Although his later career was marred by scandal, the grit, skill and flair of *El Diego* has secured his place as one of the greatest footballers of all time.

★ THE RISING STAR ★

PAULO
DYBALA

Nicknamed *La Joya* ('The Jewel'), this tricky Juventus forward is seen by many as the heir to Messi's crown. The 24-year-old was Juve's top scorer in his first season, and has a growing collection of domestic medals with the Serie A giants. Dybala has found goals harder to come by at international level, but will be desperate to put that right if given a chance in Russia.

DID YOU KNOW?

Argentina and France are the only two countries to have won all three men's global international football tournaments: the World Cup, the Confederations Cup and the Olympics.

★ THE RISING STAR ★

HÖRDUR BJÖRGVIN MAGNÚSSON

This Reykjavik-born defender regularly uses all six feet three inches of his height to his advantage, as seen when he scored a last-gasp header against Croatia during Iceland's qualifying campaign. After travelling to France for Euro 2016, he transferred from Italian giants Juventus to English Championship side Bristol City, where he's become a key part of the back line.

DID YOU KNOW?

During Euro 2016, Iceland's fans became famous for their 'Viking war cry', a slow handclap accompanied by a booming chant. However, the cry actually comes from Scotland. It was performed by Motherwell fans during a 2014 Europa League match against Icelandic club Stjarnan. The Stjarnan fans were so impressed that they took the chant home.

ICELAND

Making their first-ever World Cup appearance, Iceland – with its population of just 335,000 – is officially the smallest nation ever to qualify. Two years on from reaching the quarter-finals of Euro 2016, *Strákarnir okkar* ('Our Boys') upset the odds yet again to top their World Cup qualifying group and march on to Russia.

WORLD CUP NUMBERS

ATTENDED	0
GAMES PLAYED	0
WIN PERCENTAGE	0%
WORLD CUPS WON	0
MILES TO MOSCOW	▶ 2,054

MOST CAPS 104	MOST GOALS 26
RÚNAR KRISTINSSON	EIDUR GUDJOHNSEN

THEIR GREATEST MOMENT

= UEFA EURO 2016 =

At their first major international tournament, Iceland achieved one of football's greatest-ever shocks. After finishing above Portugal in the group stage, they pulled off a historic 2–1 win over England in the round of 16. Their adventure came to an end when hosts France beat them 5–2 in the quarter-finals – but that didn't stop 33,000 people lining the streets of Reykjavik to welcome them home as heroes. That's roughly 10 per cent of Iceland's entire population.

Position: Forward
Caps: 88 (1996–2016)
Goals: 26
Clubs: Valur, PSV, KR Reykjavík, Bolton Wanderers (twice), Chelsea, Barcelona, Monaco, Tottenham Hotspur, Stoke City, Fulham, AEK Athens, Cercle Brugge, Club Brugge, Shijiazhuang Ever Bright, Molde

THE LEGEND
EIDUR GUDJOHNSEN

Having won the Champions League and La Liga with Barcelona, plus two Premier League titles with Chelsea, Iceland's record goalscorer Guðjohnsen topped off a wonderful career by helping take his national side on their remarkable run through Euro 2016. It's perhaps his spell at Chelsea that he's best known for. After joining them from Bolton, he played over 180 times for the Blues and became an iconic figure at Stamford Bridge.

CROATIA

While their 1990s golden generation may be behind them, Croatia have missed only one World Cup since their 1998 debut, and remain a serious force to be reckoned with on the international scene.

WORLD CUP NUMBERS

ATTENDED	4
GAMES PLAYED	16
WIN PERCENTAGE	44%
WORLD CUPS WON	0
MILES TO MOSCOW	1,162

MOST CAPS	134	MOST GOALS	45
DARIJO SRNA		DAVOR ŠUKER	

THEIR GREATEST MOMENT
1998 WORLD CUP

Croatia were on a roll in 1998. After reaching the quarter-finals of Euro 1996, they arrived in France high on confidence and blessed with talent. They won group matches against Jamaica and Japan and then took out Romania before thrashing Germany 3–0 in the quarter-finals. In the end it took the momentum of hosts France to defeat them in the semi-finals and end Croatia's very real dream of winning the tournament. They consoled themselves with bronze, beating the Netherlands 2–1 in the third-place play-off match.

Position: Defender
Caps: 134 (2002–16)
Goals: 22
Clubs: Hajduk Split, Shakhtar Donetsk

11

THE LEGEND
DARIJO
SRNA

Over the course of a 14-year international career, Srna played in two World Cups and four Euros, including Croatia's run to the quarter-finals of Euro 2008. No other Croatian player even comes close to matching his 134 caps, and his 22 goals are none too shabby for a right-back either. Much of his club glory came at Shakhtar Donetsk, where he won nine Ukrainian titles and a UEFA Cup (and was Man of the Match in the 2009 final).

★ **THE RISING STAR** ★

MARKO
ROG

This 22-year-old attacking midfielder learned his trade in Croatia's lower leagues, before clinching a move to Dinamo Zagreb and then switching to Italian big-hitters Napoli. He only played once at Euro 2016 but, two years on, will be hoping for the chance to make an impact at the World Cup.

DID YOU KNOW?

Though Croatia wasn't officially part of FIFA until 1992, an unofficial Croatian side was active from 1990 and won its first game 2–1 against the USA. The team's iconic red-and-white chequered kit – based on Croatia's coat of arms – was used even then, and has been worn ever since.

★ THE RISING STAR ★

ALEX IWOBI

Nephew of Nigerian legend Jay-Jay Okocha, Alex Iwobi signed for Arsenal's academy while still at primary school, and made his first-team debut at the age of 19. Having represented England at U16, U17 and U18 levels, the Lagos-born forward switched allegiances to Nigeria – and went on to score the goal against Zambia that sent the Super Eagles to Russia.

DID YOU KNOW?

At U17 level, Nigeria rules the world. They have won the U16/U17 World Cup five times, which is more than any other nation. They have also been runners-up three times, and hold the record for scoring the most goals in a single year of the tournament (26 goals in 7 matches in 2013).

NIGERIA

Nigeria's mid-1990s golden era saw them reach the World Cup's second round in both 1994 and 1998, as well as winning the 1994 African Cup of Nations and the 1996 Olympics. As the first African team to reach Russia, the Super Eagles now have their sights set on becoming the first-ever African side to go beyond the quarter-finals.

WORLD CUP NUMBERS

ATTENDED	5
GAMES PLAYED	18
WIN PERCENTAGE	28%
WORLD CUPS WON	0
MILES TO MOSCOW	3,622

MOST CAPS 101	MOST GOALS 37
VINCENT ENYEAMA & JOSEPH YOBO	RASHIDI YEKINI

THEIR GREATEST MOMENT
=1996 OLYMPIC GAMES=

Two years on from their World Cup debut at USA 1994, Nigeria returned to the States for the Olympic Games in Atlanta. Their now-legendary run saw this exciting young side beat Hungary, Japan and Mexico to set up a semi-final against the mighty Brazil. All hope seemed lost as Nigeria went 3–1 down, but they went on to claw back a historic 4–3 victory. A dramatic final saw the Super Eagles defeat Argentina 3–2 to win gold. Back home, bars famously ran out of supplies as all-night parties broke out across the country.

Position: Forward
Caps: 87 (1994–2011)
Goals: 12
Clubs: Iwuanyanwu Nationale, Ajax, Inter Milan, Arsenal, West Bromwich Albion, Portsmouth

THE LEGEND

NWANKWO
KANU

The iconic Nwankwo Kanu isn't just an African football legend, but a classic pub quiz answer. Who's the only player to have won the Champions League, the Premier League, the UEFA Cup, the FA Cup and also been relegated from the Premier League? Now you know. Following his move from Ajax to Inter Milan in 1996, a young Kanu was diagnosed with a serious heart defect, and yet still went on to become his country's most decorated footballer. After playing in three World Cups and five African Cup of Nations, he retired from football to set up a foundation helping underprivileged children living with heart conditions across Africa.

EPIC
UNDERDOGS

The World Cup pits the game's biggest and best against each other to determine who is truly the greatest team on Earth. But it's often the exploits of the smaller nations that really stick in the memory.

NORTH KOREA

World Cup: *England 1966*
Reached: *Quarter-finals*

Even getting into England was an uphill battle for North Korea in 1966. The UK government's refusal to recognize them as a country meant they were initially blocked from entering. Fortunately, FIFA intervened and *Chollima* ('Thousand-mile horse'), as they're known, were allowed in just in time for their matches in Middlesbrough.

After starting badly with a 3–0 defeat to the Soviet Union, a mini-revival saw them earn a respectable 1–1 draw with Chile. By the time of their final group match against Italy, they'd won the hearts of Middlesbrough and the locals had well and truly adopted North Korea as their side. No one gave them a chance against the might of the Italians – but then something incredible happened. Late in the first half, Pak Doo-ik put his side 1–0 up, and it was a lead

they clung on to for the rest of the match. Italy manager Edmondo Fabbri was sacked, while Pak, a corporal in his national army, was promoted to sergeant.

North Korea (and 3,000 Middlesbrough locals who travelled to Everton's Goodison Park to cheer them on) marched on to the quarter-finals to face Portugal and the legendary Eusébio. As with the Italy match, North Korea hadn't read the script.

Within just 25 minutes, North Korea were 3–0 up and looked on course to achieve the unthinkable. That was until Portugal came to life and scored five goals to seal the tie – but it was the North Koreans who left with the standing ovation.

No one could sum up North Korea's 1966 journey better than Pak Doo-ik himself. Returning to England in 2002, he said: *'It was the day I learnt football is not all about winning. When I scored that goal, the people of Middlesbrough took us to their hearts. I learnt that playing football can improve diplomatic relations and promote peace.'* Amen to that.

▼ North Korea (in white) greet the crowd at Goodison Park before their edge-of-the-seat quarter-final against Portugal.

URUGUAY

World Cup: *Brazil 1950*
Reached: *Final round*

Despite winning the first World Cup in 1930, no one gave Uruguay a chance 20 years later. This time, there were more teams competing, Uruguay didn't have home advantage and the hosts were firm favourites.

Even when they made it to the deciding match against Brazil at the Maracanã stadium, no one thought *La Celeste* ('The Sky Blue') had a hope. In fact, the hosts were so sure they were destined for the cup that some early editions of Brazilian newspapers hit the streets declaring victory shortly after half-time.

When Brazil went one goal up in the 47th minute, the rest of the second half was seen as a mere formality. Gold medals had already been pressed for the hosts, and the victory song was being cued up. Pride comes before a fall.

In the 66th minute, Juan Alberto Schiaffino equalized. Then, with 11 minutes to go, Alcides Ghiggia netted Uruguay's winner to take Brazil's dream back to Montevideo. Ghiggia would later come out with one of the most memorable quotes in World Cup history: *'Three people have managed to silence the Maracanã – the Pope, Frank Sinatra and me.'*

▲ In front of a gigantic crowd of almost 200,000, Juan Alberto Schiaffino drills home Uruguay's equalizer in the 1950 final round.

DID YOU KNOW?

The 1950 World Cup is the only one not to have had a proper final. Instead, the top four teams entered a final group stage. Going into their match against each other, Brazil had one point more than Uruguay, so only needed a draw to win the trophy.

SOUTH KOREA

World Cup: *S. Korea & Japan 2002*
Reached: *Semi-finals*

In 2002, Guus Hiddink's South Korea took home advantage to a whole new level.

By the end of the group stage they'd already surpassed all expectations. This was a nation that had never won a World Cup match before, suddenly brushing aside Poland and Portugal (and drawing with the United States) to top their table by three points.

When they were drawn to face Italy in the round of 16, fan fever escalated. City centres across the country were awash with seas of red, watching 'The Red Devils' on giant public screens. However, after missing an early penalty and then going a goal down, it looked like

the end of the line. That was until the 88th minute, when Seol Ki-hyeon equalized to send the tie into extra-time.

With the Italians in disarray (partly due to some highly contentious refereeing decisions), Ahn Jung-hwan headed home to put his nation in the quarter-finals and himself, ironically, out of work (his Italian club, Perugia, fired him for scoring the goal that killed Italy's World Cup dream).

Next up was Spain. Millions of Koreans gathered together to watch live public screenings, desperate fans parted with over £1,700 for tickets, and there were even calls for Hiddink to run for president.

Again there was controversial refereeing, again there were penalties involved, and again South

Korea prevailed. With the match goalless after extra-time, the Red Devils won the shootout to become the first Asian country ever to reach the World Cup semi-finals.

Legend has it that by this stage doctors were being inundated with patients suffering from hoarse voices and throat pains, while other fans were hospitalized with wrist injuries caused by excessive clapping and flag-waving.

But even the best parties come to an end, and it was ultimately Germany who brought a halt to this one. Michael Ballack's 75th-minute goal was enough to separate the sides in the semi, and there was to be no World Cup final for South Korea. However, the Koreans had cemented their place in football history, and Hiddink was honoured with Korean citizenship.

▼ South Korea fans transform Seoul's City Plaza into a breath-taking sea of red and white following their team's dramatic quarter-final win over Spain in 2002. Over seven million Koreans (around one-seventh of the population) would flock to outdoor screens to watch the semi-final against Germany.

SEOUL WELCOMES THE WORLD

NEW ZEALAND

World Cup: *South Africa 2010*
Reached: *Group stage*

The 2010 World Cup treated us to some wonderful sides at the very peak of their powers.

But there was just one team that made it through the tournament undefeated. It wasn't Ronaldo's Portugal, or reigning champions Italy, or even eventual winners Spain. It was Oceanic minnows New Zealand, who shook the football world over the course of three group matches.

First up was Slovakia, and a 1–1 draw thanks to Winston Reid's equalizer deep into added time. That cued up a huge match against Marcello Lippi's star-studded Italy team. Seven minutes in, Shane Smeltz gave the All Whites an unlikely lead. Vincenzo Iaquinta equalized for the Italians, but his side had to make do with a point as New Zealand held firm at the back.

New Zealand's third and final match was also a 1–1 draw – this time against a formidable Paraguay side who would go on to reach the quarter-finals.

While it wasn't enough to get the All Whites into the next round, they earned a newfound support back home, in a country more known for its love of rugby.

USA

World Cup: *Brazil 1950*
Reached: *Group stage*

One was the birthplace of the modern game, boasting a team filled with stars such as Alf Ramsey, Tom Finney and Billy Wright. The other was a squad of mailmen, railway workers and miners.

So, when England lined up against the USA in the group stage, the question was not who would win, but by how much would England win. What happened next remains one of the biggest shocks in World Cup history.

A scrappy 37th-minute goal from American-Haitian dishwasher Joe Gaetjens gave the USA a lead that they wouldn't relinquish, and 1–0 was how it finished. The amateurs had beaten the professionals.

The USA lost their next match 5–2 to Chile and didn't make it out of the group stage, but they had already secured their place in football folklore.

DID YOU KNOW?

Urban myth has it that several English newspapers reported the score as being 10–1 to England, as they thought the USA's 1–0 win must have been a typo. However, there's no surviving evidence that this ever actually happened.

▶ American goalkeeper Frank Borghi saves to keep out England's Tom Finney.

THE BEST OF THE REST

Here are some of the other great underdog stories that didn't make our list.

West Germany, 1954
It wouldn't seem unusual today, but West Germany's triumph over Hungary to win the final – known as 'The Miracle of Bern' – was a major upset at the time. There's more on this on page 116.

Algeria, 1982
In their first-ever World Cup match, Algeria turned up and beat hotly fancied West Germany 2–1. In the process, they became the first African side to beat a European nation in the World Cup.

Cameroon, 1990
Cameroon's march to the quarter-finals, defeating Argentina, Romania and Colombia along the way, remains one of football's greatest fairy-tales.

Bulgaria, 1994
Iordan Letchkov's diving header against Germany to send Bulgaria into the semis remains one of the most enduring images of USA 1994.

Senegal, 2002
It's the opening match. France are the reigning champions. Senegal are the newbies. Papa Bouba Diop scores the only goal of the game, and the rest is history.

◀ Bulgaria's USA 1994 heroes celebrate ditching Germany out of the tournament to march into a semi-final clash against Brazil. It eventually took a solitary Romário goal to prevent them from going all the way to the final.

BRAZIL

They're the only nation to have appeared at every single World Cup, and have lifted the trophy more times than any other nation. With their talisman Neymar leading the way, the Brazilians head to the World Cup – as always – as one of the big favourites.

WORLD CUP NUMBERS

ATTENDED	20
GAMES PLAYED	104
WIN PERCENTAGE	67%
WORLD CUPS WON	★★★★★ 5
MILES TO MOSCOW	▶ 7,169

MOST CAPS  148	MOST GOALS 77
CAFU	PELÉ

THEIR GREATEST MOMENT
= 1970 WORLD CUP =

On a sweltering day in Mexico City, Italy and Brazil met, knowing one of them would become the first country to win three World Cups. A 4–1 victory for the rampant Brazilians left no doubt over which side was truly the greatest. The iconic moment came with four minutes to go, when Pelé calmly passed the ball to Carlos Alberto who powered it into the far corner of the net for one of the finest goals ever scored. Nearly 50 years later, that 1970 squad is still considered by many to be the greatest football team of all time. The class of 2018 has a lot to live up to.

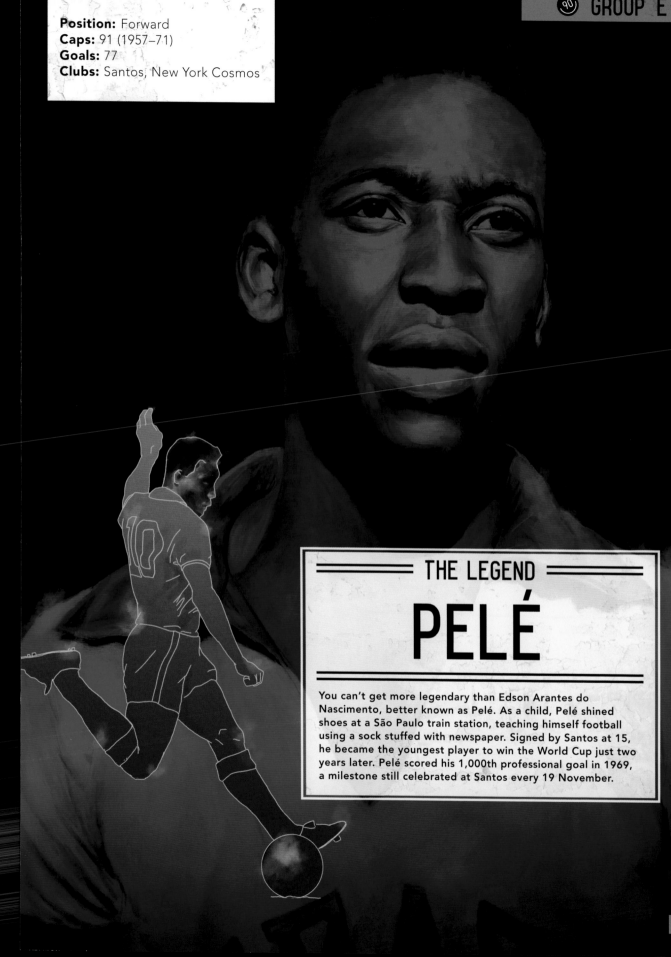

Position: Forward
Caps: 91 (1957–71)
Goals: 77
Clubs: Santos, New York Cosmos

THE LEGEND

PELÉ

You can't get more legendary than Edson Arantes do Nascimento, better known as Pelé. As a child, Pelé shined shoes at a São Paulo train station, teaching himself football using a sock stuffed with newspaper. Signed by Santos at 15, he became the youngest player to win the World Cup just two years later. Pelé scored his 1,000th professional goal in 1969, a milestone still celebrated at Santos every 19 November.

★ **THE RISING STAR** ★

GABRIEL

JESUS

The Manchester City forward has come a long way from playing barefoot on the concrete football pitches of São Paulo. Making his debut for Palmeiras in March 2015, the gifted striker would go on to win gold at the 2016 Olympics in Rio, before scoring two goals against Ecuador in his first match for the senior team just one month later. At least one footballing legend, Brazil's own Ronaldinho, has gone on record to say that Jesus could become the best footballer in the world.

DID YOU KNOW?

Brazil is the only football team to have won the World Cup on four different continents. That's once in Asia, South America and Europe, and twice in North America.

★ THE RISING STAR ★

BREEL
EMBOLO

Cameroon-born Embolo made his first-team debut for Basel at 17 years old and, incredibly, was playing Champions League games while still at school. After playing for Switzerland at Euro 2016, the quick and powerful striker made the move to Germany's Bundesliga, signing for Schalke for a fee in the region of £20 million. The 2018 World Cup could well be the time for this 21-year-old to make a big name for himself.

DID YOU KNOW?

In 2006, Switzerland became the first team to be knocked out of the World Cup without conceding a goal. They topped their group with clean sheets against France, Togo and South Korea, and were eventually eliminated on penalties after drawing 0–0 with Ukraine in the round of 16.

SWITZERLAND

It's 64 years since Switzerland last made it as far as the World Cup quarter-finals. Then, they were the hosts of the 1954 edition. Today, Russia will welcome the strongest Swiss side in decades, with a squad made up of players from across some of Europe's best leagues.

WORLD CUP NUMBERS

ATTENDED	10
GAMES PLAYED	33
WIN PERCENTAGE	33%
WORLD CUPS WON	0
MILES TO MOSCOW	1,504

MOST CAPS 🧢 118	MOST GOALS ⚽ 42
HEINZ HERMANN	ALEXANDER FREI

THEIR GREATEST MOMENT

= 1954 WORLD CUP =

As hosts, Switzerland made it through a tough group stage before taking on Austria in a quarter-final that turned out to be one of the most exciting games in World Cup history. The Swiss took the lead early on and scored three goals in the first 19 minutes. But the goals kept coming, at both ends of the pitch. Switzerland added another two goals to their tally, but amazingly still ended up losing 7–5. It was the end of Switzerland's involvement in the tournament, but they went out on a high.

Position: Forward
Caps: 103 (1989–2004)
Goals: 21
Clubs: Malley, Lausanne (twice), Bayer 05 Uerdingen, Borussia Dortmund, Grasshopper Club Zürich, BSC Young Boys

THE LEGEND
STÉPHANE
CHAPUISAT

Switzerland had been absent from the World Cup for 28 years when Stéphane Chapuisat scored six of the vital qualifying goals that sent his country to USA 1994. With a consistently high work-rate, the four-time Swiss Footballer of the Year scored 106 times in 230 appearances for Borussia Dortmund, making him one of only six foreign players to score over a hundred goals in the German Bundesliga.

COSTA RICA

Los Ticos were one of the surprise packages of the last World Cup, beating Uruguay, Italy and Greece on their march to the quarter-finals. If they match that run in Russia, it'll go down as an even bigger shock.

WORLD CUP NUMBERS

ATTENDED	4
GAMES PLAYED	15
WIN PERCENTAGE	33%
WORLD CUPS WON	0
MILES TO MOSCOW	6,818

MOST CAPS	🧢 135	MOST GOALS	⚽ 47
WALTER CENTENO		**ROLANDO FONSECA**	

THEIR GREATEST MOMENT
= 2014 WORLD CUP =

On paper, the odds of Costa Rica winning the 2014 World Cup were a distinctly unlikely 2,500 to 1. However, that didn't stop Jorge Luis Pinto's fast, exciting group of players from topping their group, knocking out Greece in the round of 16 and then giving the Netherlands a major scare in the quarter-finals. It took a nail-biting penalty shootout to send the Dutch through, but it was arguably the Costa Ricans who stole the watching world's hearts.

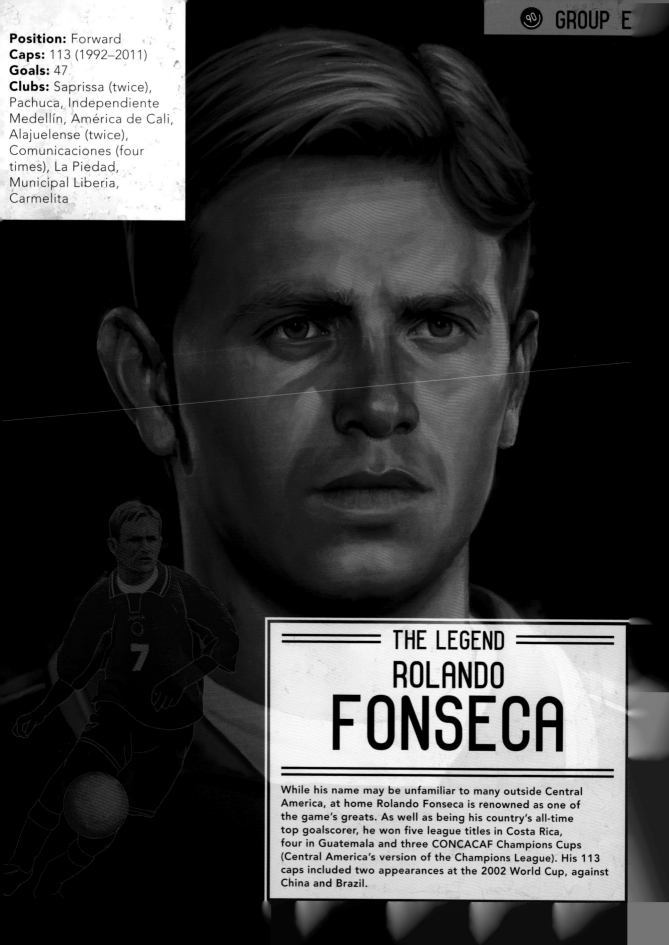

Position: Forward
Caps: 113 (1992–2011)
Goals: 47
Clubs: Saprissa (twice), Pachuca, Independiente Medellín, América de Cali, Alajuelense (twice), Comunicaciones (four times), La Piedad, Municipal Liberia, Carmelita

THE LEGEND
ROLANDO
FONSECA

While his name may be unfamiliar to many outside Central America, at home Rolando Fonseca is renowned as one of the game's greats. As well as being his country's all-time top goalscorer, he won five league titles in Costa Rica, four in Guatemala and three CONCACAF Champions Cups (Central America's version of the Champions League). His 113 caps included two appearances at the 2002 World Cup, against China and Brazil.

THE RISING STAR ★

RÓNALD

MATARRITA

...ng full-back has hit the
...running since moving from his
...own side of Alajuelense to MLS
...ers New York City FC in 2016.
...rst season, he was named his
...b's Defensive Player of the
...d became a fixture for his
...l side. A powerful presence
...he left-hand side, the
...-old has gained plaudits for
...s attacking and defensive play.

DID YOU KNOW?

There are seven nations in Central America, but Costa Rica are the only one to have ever won a match at the World Cup . . . so far.

THE RISING STAR ★

ALEKSANDAR
MITROVIC

notching up six goals during World Cup qualifiers (making him scorer in the group), Newcastle r Mitrović has emerged as a's key goal threat at just 23 of age. Before his call-up to the r team, he was named player of ournament in Serbia's victorious U19 Championship in 2013.

SERBIA

Serbia played their first match as an independent state back in 2006, but are the successors to the Yugoslavia and Serbia & Montenegro sides whose proud history dates all the way back to the very first World Cup in 1930, where they came fourth. Their impressive 2018 squad boasts players from all across Europe's top leagues.

WORLD CUP NUMBERS

ATTENDED	11
GAMES PLAYED	43
WIN PERCENTAGE	40%
WORLD CUPS WON	0
MILES TO MOSCOW	1,068

MOST CAPS 🧢 103	MOST GOALS ⚽ 38
DEJAN STANKOVIĆ	STJEPAN BOBEK

THEIR GREATEST MOMENT
= 2010 WORLD CUP =

While Yugoslavia enjoyed many great moments, particularly during the 1950s and 1960s, for Serbia a watershed moment came in 2010 when they qualified for their first World Cup as an independent nation. Taking on Germany, who hadn't lost a group match since 1986, Milan Jovanović scored the game's only goal to secure a historic victory. Serbia didn't make it past the group stage, but by beating one of the big favourites they had announced their arrival on the world stage.

Position: Winger
Caps: 85 (1964–78)
Goals: 23
Clubs: Red Star Belgrade (twice), SC Bastia

THE LEGEND
DRAGAN
DŽAJIĆ

Džajić was a formidable opponent on the left wing, capable of sudden bursts of speed and clever trickery. Nicknamed the 'Balkan miracle' by none other than Pelé, he banged in over 100 goals across two spells with the mighty Red Star Belgrade, winning five Yugoslavian championships along the way. The peak of his international career came at Euro 1968, where he scored two goals to help Yugoslavia finish the tournament as runners-up.

TOP TEN WORLD CUP CONTROVERSIES

90

The World Cup may be the showpiece tournament of the beautiful game, but it's seen its fair share of uproar. Here are ten moments that have stood out for all the wrong reasons . . .

10 THE BATTLE OF SANTIAGO

You'd be hard pushed to find a more violent match in World Cup history than this 1962 battle between Italy and hosts Chile. And 'battle' is very definitely the right word.

It took just 12 seconds until the first foul, and 12 minutes until the first sending off. By full-time, there had been two sendings off, a broken nose, four police interventions, punching, kicking, spitting . . . oh, and two goals for Chile (not that many people were talking about those).

The whole thing was so brutal that the BBC introduced their highlights with the warning: *'The game you are about to see is the most stupid, appalling, disgusting and disgraceful exhibition of football, possibly in the history of the game.'*

9 THE BIG RONALDO MYSTERY

This incident is wrapped in so many layers of conspiracy theory and confusion that, to this day, many remain unconvinced about what really happened.

Here's what we do know: it's the final of the 1998 World Cup between Brazil and France, and Ronaldo (the original one) represents Brazil's best hope of victory. But, when the teams are announced, flying in the face of all reasoning, Ronaldo's name is missing.

As the world's media went into meltdown, there was a late change and Brazil's star man was reinstated to the team sheet. It wasn't enough, however. Ronaldo did go on to start the game and play the full 90 minutes, but he failed to produce his electric form of the previous rounds and he and his teammates ended up getting thumped 3–0.

Amid the rumours that followed were stories about sponsor interference, a mysterious injury and even a suggestion that he had been poisoned. However, Ronaldo himself has since said that he suffered a seizure on the night before the match, but later declared himself fit to play.

▼ This Qatari fan gets the party started nice and early, in preparation for the World Cup coming to Qatar in 2022.

8 WELCOME TO QATAR

If the choice of Russia as 2018 World Cup hosts raised eyebrows, the decision to send the 2022 competition to the tiny Gulf state of Qatar caused mass uproar.

In the eight years since Qatar was awarded the tournament, there have been rows over everything from venues and stadium construction, to climate and national politics. It's been nothing if not interesting.

It has since been confirmed that, due to the extreme summer heat in Qatar, the competition will kick off in November – making it the first-ever World Cup not to be played in May, June or July.

7 THE SHOOTING OF ANDRÉS ESCOBAR

Off the back of a qualification campaign that included hammering Argentina 5–0 away from home, Colombia were heavily fancied to do the business at World Cup 1994.

Unfortunately, the reality didn't quite match up to the expectations. Defender Andrés Escobar scored an own goal in his side's second game, a 2–1 defeat by the USA that would effectively send the Colombians crashing out of the tournament.

Upon the team's return to Colombia, Escobar was tragically shot dead outside a bar in his home city of Medellín. The shooter apparently shouted 'goal' with each of the bullets fired at him. Today, a statue of Escobar stands in Medellín.

6 THE HAMMERING OF PERU

Back in the day – or, in this case, 1978 – the World Cup second round consisted of two groups of four teams, with the winner of each group advancing to the final.

Ahead of their last group match, hosts Argentina needed to beat Copa América-holders Peru by four clear goals to reach the final ahead of bitter rivals Brazil.

The half-time score was 2–0 to Argentina, but a second-half collapse from the Peruvians saw Argentina romp to a 6–0 victory. While no wrongdoing was ever proven, rumours of foul play quickly spread around the globe. The fact that Peru's goalkeeper was born in Argentina probably didn't help.

5 THE DISGRACE OF GIJÓN

Surely the most pathetic game in World Cup history was this one between neighbouring countries West Germany and Austria in Gijón, Spain, at World Cup 1982.

The group sat on a knife-edge after the other two sides in the group – Algeria and Chile – played their final group match the day before. So . . . a German win by three or more goals would eliminate Austria; a draw or an Austrian win would eliminate West Germany; but a German victory by one or two goals would send both countries through. You still with us?

Ten minutes into the match, the Germans went 1–0 up, effectively meaning that both sides would qualify for the next round if nothing changed. And so, for the next 80 minutes, the two sides went into autopilot, passing the ball around between themselves, barely making any tackles and making hardly any effort to score.

The match finished 1–0, both countries progressed and Algeria crashed out of the tournament. The watching world was far from impressed.

DID YOU KNOW?

As a direct result of 'The Disgrace of Gijón', the rule was introduced that the final pair of matches in each group must always kick-off at the same time.

4 SOUTH KOREA'S ROAD TO THE SEMIS

As co-hosts of the 2002 World Cup, South Korea rode a wave of global goodwill all the way to the semi-finals – enchanting the watching world in the process. But there were plenty of eyebrows raised among conspiracy theorists along the way.

Against Italy in the round of 16, the Koreans caused a major upset by winning 2–1 after extra-time. However, the referee was on the receiving end of no shortage of criticism for some of his decisions – notably disallowing an Italian goal in extra-time on a questionable offside call, and then showing Francesco Totti a second yellow for diving when it looked like he'd been fouled.

South Korea went on to cause another shock in the quarter-finals, this time holding Spain to a 0–0 draw before going through on penalties. But again, a big question mark hung over the ref's performance and two Spanish goals were disallowed.

For more on South Korea's remarkable World Cup adventure in 2002, turn to page 89.

▼ Italy's Angelo Di Livio has a quiet word with the ref during his side's shock exit to South Korea in 2002.

▲ 'The Hand of Diego Maradona' . . . also known as 'The Hand of God'.

3 ZIZOU'S HEADBUTT

Zinedine 'Zizou' Zidane was at the height of his powers at the 2006 World Cup. He led France, virtually single-handedly, to the final against Italy – only to ruin his tournament with a moment of madness.

With the match locked at 1–1 deep into extra-time, Zizou went from hero to zero as he inexplicably headbutted Italy's Marco Materazzi in the chest and got himself sent off. The reason? Materazzi had mocked Zidane's mother/sister (depending on whose version of events you believe).

Italy would go on to win 5–3 on penalties. And, to rub salt into Zidane's wounds, Materazzi was among the scorers.

> **DID YOU KNOW?**
>
> Only four other players have ever been sent off in a World Cup final: France's Marcel Desailly (1998); Argentina's Pedro Monzón and Gustavo Dezotti (both in 1990); Netherlands' Johnny Heitinga (2010).

2 HURST'S HAT-TRICK

England's third goal against West Germany in the 1966 final provides an early example of a time when goal-line technology would have come in handy.

Eleven minutes into extra-time, with the match poised at 2–2, English striker Geoff Hurst fired a shot that hit the underside of the crossbar, bounced down and was cleared away. Unsure if the ball had crossed the line, the ref looked to his linesman, a Soviet named Tofik Bakhramov, and the goal was given.

But did it really go in? Recent video analysis strongly suggests that yes, it did. However, Bakhramov would later say that he thought the ball had bounced back off the net, not the crossbar, so it turns out that even he wasn't sure.

Not that England cared. Hurst went on to score again to secure a historic 4–2 Wembley win for the hosts. To this day, he remains the only player to score a hat-trick in a World Cup final.

1 THE HAND OF GOD

In the 1986 World Cup, Argentina faced England in the quarter-finals. Six minutes into the second half, a misplaced clearance saw the ball loop up into the England box.

With an 8-inch height advantage, it should have been easy pickings for goalkeeper Peter Shilton – but Diego Maradona had other ideas. The Argentine legend leaped up beside Shilton and punched the ball into the back of the net to put his side 1–0 up.

Despite the England players' protests, referee Ali Bin Nasser was unmoved and allowed the illegal goal to stand. It would prove to be a pivotal moment in a match (and a tournament) that Argentina went on to win.

Maradona himself cheekily coined the term 'The Hand of God' in the post-match press conference – and it's a name that's stuck ever since.

TOP FIVE GREATEST PERFORMANCES

90

Football may be a team game, but it's often the individual moments of magic that truly stick in the memory. Here are five players whose solo performances will forever be the stuff of World Cup legend.

5 ZINEDINE ZIDANE ■ ■ *Brazil v. FRANCE, Stade de France (Paris, France), 1998*

'Zizou' was never one to shy away from the big stage. The French midfield legend was pivotal in France's 3–0 victory over Brazil in the final of 1998, scoring two goals and picking up the man-of-the-match award.

4 EUSÈBIO 🇵🇹 *PORTUGAL v. North Korea, Goodison Park (Liverpool, England), 1966*

Years before a certain Cristiano Ronaldo entered the scene, history was being written by another one of Portugal's all-time greats: Eusébio. During the 1966 World Cup, the Portuguese faced an unlikely opponent in North Korea. Against all odds, the North Koreans took a 3–0 lead after just 25 minutes. It would have been an upset of huge proportions . . . were it not for one man. Eusébio took the game by the scruff of the neck and scored four goals in quick succession. José Augusto added a late fifth goal to the tally, giving the Portuguese a 5–3 win and a place in the quarter-finals. Eusébio finished the tournament as top scorer with nine goals to his name.

3 PELÈ 🇧🇷 *BRAZIL v. Sweden, Råsunda Stadium (Solna, Sweden), 1958*

Talk about making your mark on the world stage! Pelé was just 17 when he set the World Cup alight with this iconic performance. After driving his side to the final with a goal against Wales in the quarters and a cool hat-trick against France in the semis, he went on to become the youngest-ever scorer in a World Cup final with a double against host nation Sweden. No player so young has made such an impact at a World Cup since, and it's hard to imagine it happening again.

2 DIEGO MARADONA 🇦🇷 *ARGENTINA v. England, Estadio Azteca (Mexico City, Mexico), 1986*

His 'Hand of God' moment tops our list of controversies (see page 111), and his all-round performance in that same match comes close to topping this one. This game is up there with the best in World Cup history . . . and that's all down to this guy. Minutes after punching the ball beyond Peter Shilton and into the England net, he went on a mazy run and calmly slotted the ball home, sending his side surging into the lead. It was Maradona 2 England 1, and World Cup history was written. Maradona was simply one of the best footballers ever to grace the game (even when using his hand), and this was arguably his finest hour-and-a-half.

1 GEOFF HURST ➕ *ENGLAND v. West Germany, Wembley Stadium (London, England), 1966*

Hurst only made his international debut in February 1966, yet just a few months later he was representing his country in the World Cup final. Sir Geoff slotted past goalkeeper Hans Tilkowski three times on the day, earning himself the match ball and winning a first – and, so far, only – World Cup for England.

Find out more about Geoff Hurst's controversial hat-trick on page 111.

◄ Geoff Hurst heads goalwards to make it 1–1 in the 1966 final in front of 97,000 fans at the old Wembley Stadium.

TOP FIVE NIGHTMARE PERFORMANCES

90

Of course, not every player who goes to the World Cup experiences glory and adulation. Here are five moments the guilty parties would prefer to forget . . . but never will.

5 ROBERTO BAGGIO
Brazil v. ITALY, Rose Bowl (Pasadena, United States), 1994

Italians and penalties: a foregone conclusion, right? Wrong. It's the World Cup final, we're deep into a penalty shootout, and Italy's talismanic hero Baggio has the chance to draw his side level with Brazil. Agonizingly, he steps up and blazes the ball over the bar, instantly handing the trophy to the Brazilians. Baggio was one of the greatest players of his era and one of the players of the tournament, but he'll forever be remembered for this heartbreaking spot-kick.

4 GRAHAM POLL
Croatia v. Australia, Gottlieb-Daimler-Stadion (Stuttgart, Germany), 2006

OK, so he's not actually a player, but there's no way Graham Poll could be left off this list. If players and teams are lambasted for dire World Cup performances, spare a thought for referees. In 2006, this English ref was disgraced and sent home after brandishing three yellow cards to the same player in one game! Croatia's Josip Šimunić was the player on the receiving end of Poll's blunder, picking up three bookings before finally being sent for an early (but not early enough) bath. It was Poll's first major mistake in 26 years of refereeing, but it was still enough for him to be sent packing.

3 DAVID BECKHAM
Argentina v. ENGLAND, Stade Geoffroy-Guichard (Saint-Étienne, France), 1998

Boy wonder turned bad. This is the moment that Beckham himself will never forget, and for all the wrong reasons. After being fouled by pantomime villain Diego Simeone, Beckham petulantly kicked out at the Argentinian while still lying on the ground. Not only was Becks sent off, he was tormented by the English press for weeks on end. Ten-man England crashed out of the tournament on penalties, and Beckham was an easy scapegoat.

2 JOSEPH MWEPU ILUNGA
ZAIRE v. Brazil, Waldstadion (Frankfurt, West Germany), 1974

This has to be one of the strangest moments in World Cup history. During the final Group B match, Brazil winger Jairzinho was about to take a free-kick when Zaire defender Ilunga broke from the six-man wall, ran up to the ball and smashed it up the pitch. What was he thinking? All became apparent years later when Ilunga admitted it was an act of protest against the Zairian authorities. He'd hoped to be sent off – but the ref was lenient and he only saw yellow.

1 LUIS SUÁREZ 🇺🇾 *URUGUAY v. Ghana, Soccer City (Johannesburg, South Africa), 2010*

He's the player you love to hate and, in 2010, Suárez was back in football's bad books. With the edge-of-the-seat quarter-final poised at 1–1 deep in extra-time, Dominic Adiyiah sent a header towards the Uruguayan goal only for Suárez to block it on the line with his hands. Devastatingly for Ghana, Asamoah Gyan then missed the resultant penalty and Uruguay went on to win the shootout. Ghanaian hearts were broken, and Mr Suárez was once again making the wrong sorts of headlines.

▲ Luis Suárez uses his hands to keep out Ghana in the 2010 quarter-finals. Despite being sent off, he hung around by the pitch just long enough to celebrate the penalty miss that followed.

GERMANY

Returning to defend the trophy they won in Brazil in 2014, Germany have qualified for every World Cup they've ever entered. It's little wonder the four-time champions are known as simply *Die Mannschaft* ('The Team').

WORLD CUP NUMBERS

ATTENDED	18
GAMES PLAYED	106
WIN PERCENTAGE	62%
WORLD CUPS WON	★★★★ 4
MILES TO MOSCOW	▶ 1,001

MOST CAPS	150
LOTHAR MATTHÄUS	

MOST GOALS	71
MIROSLAV KLOSE	

THEIR GREATEST MOMENT
= 1954 WORLD CUP =

It's not often that the Germans have been considered underdogs, but no one gave West Germany a hope of winning the 1954 World Cup final in Switzerland. Opponents Hungary had already thrashed them 8–3 in the group stage, and hadn't lost a game in four years. True to form, within just eight minutes, the favourites went 2–0 up. And yet, incredibly, the underdogs came back to win 3–2, in what is known to this day as 'The Miracle of Bern'. Almost fifty years later, in 2003, the story of the match was even turned into a movie.

Position: Defender
Caps: 103 (1965–77)
Goals: 14
Clubs: Bayern Munich, New York Cosmos (twice), Hamburger SV

THE LEGEND
FRANZ
BECKENBAUER

Dubbed *Der Kaiser* ('The Emperor'), this classy sweeper is one of the most decorated and acclaimed footballers in history. He won Germany's Bundesliga five times, the German Cup four times, the European Cup three times, the World Cup once, the Euros once, and a whole host of other gongs including the Ballon d'Or twice and four German Footballer of the Year awards. Even retirement couldn't stop him from winning. As a manager, he won another World Cup, France's Ligue 1 title with Marseille, the UEFA Cup and another Bundesliga with Bayern Munich. Now that's a CV.

★ THE RISING STAR ★

TIMO WERNER

RB Leipzig parted with a record transfer fee of around €10 million to take this frontman from Bundesliga rivals Stuttgart – and what a piece of business that turned out to be. His 21 goals in season 2016/17 made him the league's top German scorer, and he secured his place in Germany's squad for the 2017 Confederations Cup, where he scooped the Golden Boot award. Werner looks destined to be the latest in a long and impressive line of deadly German forwards.

DID YOU KNOW?

Germany are the undisputed kings of the World Cup penalty shootout. They have played four, won four, and only missed a single shot from the spot since the very first shootout against France in 1982.

★ THE RISING STAR ★

EDSON ÁLVAREZ

Edson Álvarez has enjoyed a meteoric rise since making his Liga MX debut with Club América in 2016. At just 19 years of age, the towering centre-back featured for his country in last year's CONCACAF Gold Cup, becoming Mexico's youngest player ever to score in the tournament. Expect scouts to be keeping close tabs on him if he appears in Russia.

DID YOU KNOW?

La Ola – better known as the Mexican Wave – became an international phenomenon at the 1986 World Cup. To this day, it's a common sight among crowds at events all over the world – often when there's not much else to get excited about!

MEXICO

El Tri (short for *El Tricolor*) have been at every World Cup since 1994, but haven't made it past the round of 16 in any of them. Having comfortably topped their qualifying group, a strong run to the latter stages of the tournament is surely long overdue.

WORLD CUP NUMBERS

ATTENDED	15
GAMES PLAYED	53
WIN PERCENTAGE	26%
WORLD CUPS WON	0
MILES TO MOSCOW	6,668

MOST CAPS 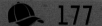 177	MOST GOALS 49
CLAUDIO SUÁREZ	JAVIER HERNÁNDEZ

THEIR GREATEST MOMENT
= 1986 WORLD CUP =

Although Mexico has won many CONCACAF titles, a Confederations Cup and even the Olympics, their best World Cup performance remains their march to the quarter-finals on home soil in 1986. They topped their group and put Bulgaria out of the round of 16, before eventually succumbing to West Germany on penalties.

Position: Forward
Caps: 58 (1977–94)
Goals: 29
Clubs: Universidad Nacional, San Diego Sockers, Atlético Madrid, Real Madrid, América, Rayo Vallecano, Atlante, Linz, Dallas Burn, Celaya

THE LEGEND

HUGO SÁNCHEZ

Who do you think might be the only player to top Spain's La Liga goalscoring charts four seasons in a row? Lionel Messi? Cristiano Ronaldo? How about Raúl? Nope. The answer is Hugo Sánchez. Between 1984/85 and 1987/88, he scored an incredible 104 goals in 143 appearances, and then came back to win the top-scorer award a fifth time in 1989/90. He also played in the 1986 Mexico team that went all the way to the World Cup quarter-finals. Having trained as a gymnast, Sánchez was particularly fond of a bicycle-kick, and celebrated every goal with a flamboyant somersault in honour of his sister, an Olympic gymnast in her own right.

SWEDEN

After knocking the highly favoured Italy out of the qualification play-offs, Sweden arrive in Russia knowing that, on their day, they're a match for any opponent. This is their first World Cup since making it to the round of 16 at Germany 2006.

WORLD CUP NUMBERS

ATTENDED	11
GAMES PLAYED	46
WIN PERCENTAGE	35%
WORLD CUPS WON	0
MILES TO MOSCOW	763

MOST CAPS	148
ANDERS SVENSSON	

MOST GOALS	62
ZLATAN IBRAHIMOVIĆ	

THEIR GREATEST MOMENT
= 1948 OLYMPICS =

Due to the Second World War, the 1948 Olympics was the first major international football tournament for ten years – and Sweden dominated it. Their prominence was largely thanks to the attacking threesome of Gunnar Gren, Gunnar Nordahl and Nils Liedholm, who became known collectively as 'Gre-No-Li'. The trio led the way in a series of convincing wins, including a remarkable 12–0 win over South Korea in the quarter-finals. In the gold-medal match they beat Yugoslavia 3–1 to secure what remains the only major tournament win in their history.

Position: Forward
Caps: 116 (2001–16)
Goals: 62
Clubs: Malmö, Ajax, Juventus, Inter Milan, Barcelona, AC Milan, Paris Saint-Germain, Manchester United

THE LEGEND
ZLATAN
IBRAHIMOVIĆ

One of the most decorated and iconic players of the modern game, Sweden's number-one goalscorer has won a trophy for every season of his career since 2001. He's won 13 championships in four separate countries and is the only player to score Champions League goals for six different teams. With a level of fame and adulation that goes way beyond the football pitch, Zlatan is revered in Sweden as one of the country's greatest-ever sportspeople, rivalled only by tennis legend Björn Borg.

THE RISING STAR ★

VICTOR
LINDELOF

...ng Sweden to join Portuguese
...Benfica at the age of just 17,
...eedy centre-back became
...n as the 'Iceman' due to his
...to remain cool under extreme
...ure. After starting in all three of
...en's matches at Euro 2016, he
...d to Manchester United for a
...ed £30 million. Despite a
...nging start to his career at Old
...rd, he remains a key part of his
...al team's defence.

DID YOU KNOW?

Sweden reached the semis
of the 1950 World Cup with a squad
made up entirely of amateur players.
However, after failing to qualify for 1954,
the Swedish FA decided to allow
professionals into the national team.
As hosts in 1958, Sweden's team
of pros went all the way
to the final.

★ THE RISING STAR ★

LEE

LEE SEUNG-WOO

Dubbed the Korean Messi, Lee Seung-woo was spotted by a Barcelona scout and spirited away to Catalonia at the age of just 12. After scoring 39 goals in 29 games for Barça's under-13 side – breaking a record set by Messi himself – he made his debut for Barcelona B in 2016. Now with Hellas Verona of Italy's Serie A, he wasn't capped during the qualifiers, but looks well-placed to break through in time to board the plane to Russia.

DID YOU KNOW?

There were no home and away fixtures in the early days of South Korea's K League. Instead, the five original member clubs toured the country, playing each other in front of small crowds more used to baseball. It's come a long way since then.

SOUTH KOREA

The Reds have now qualified for nine consecutive World Cups – an Asian record. However, few will give these perennial underdogs much hope of beating their best-ever finish of fourth place back in 2002.

WORLD CUP NUMBERS

ATTENDED	9
GAMES PLAYED	31
WIN PERCENTAGE	16%
WORLD CUPS WON	0
MILES TO MOSCOW	4,109

MOST CAPS	135	MOST GOALS	58
CHA BUM-KUN		CHA BUM-KUN	

THEIR GREATEST MOMENT

= 2002 WORLD CUP =

The year 2002 was when the football world took Korea to their hearts. As co-hosts, Guus Hiddink's side went from having never won a match at a World Cup to marching all the way to the semi-finals. Along the way, they took the scalps of Poland, Portugal, Italy and Spain, and it took a narrow 1–0 defeat by Germany to end their miraculous run. For one brief, glorious summer, every football fan truly wanted to 'Be the Reds'.

Position: Forward
Caps: 135 (1972–86)
Goals: 58
Clubs: Seoul Trust Bank, South Korean Air Force, SV Darmstadt 98, Eintracht Frankfurt, Bayer Leverkusen

THE LEGEND
CHA
BUM-KUN

Nicknamed 'Tscha Boom' thanks to his powerful right foot, Cha Bum-kun became the first Korean to star in a top European league when he was snapped up by German giants Eintracht Frankfurt. At the same time as conquering the Bundesliga, he was also banging in goals for his national side, and remains Korea's all-time top scorer. He managed his country at the 1998 World Cup, and in 1999 he was voted Asia's Player of the Century.

BAD BLOOD

Every country wants to win every match, but sometimes there's a little bit of history that gives a game that something extra. From on-the-pitch feuds to off-the-pitch tensions, here are ten World Cup head-to-heads that have some serious beef.

🇩🇰 DENMARK v. SWEDEN 🇸🇪

Over the last three decades, Denmark–Sweden has become something of a *clásico* of international football. The two Scandinavian nations have always been competitive with one another, but their football rivalry really got going in 1992 when they met each other in the Euros. Sweden won that game 1–0, but the Danes went on to pull off a major shock when they won the tournament itself – on Swedish soil. Fifteen years later, a Euro 2008 qualifier in Copenhagen indelibly marked this fixture. With Sweden 3–0 up, Denmark pulled off a remarkable comeback to bring it back to 3–3. In the last minute, the Swedes were awarded a dramatic penalty, but it was never taken. A Danish fan ran onto the pitch and attempted to punch the German referee. All hell broke loose, the match was abandoned and Sweden were awarded a 3–0 win. Things swung back in Denmark's favour when the sides met again in the qualifiers for the 2010 World Cup. Denmark won both matches 1–0 and marched on to the Finals in South Africa.

🇫🇷 FRANCE v. ITALY 🇮🇹

Whether it's a discussion about who has the better wine, cheese, holiday destinations or football players, it's never been easy to decide who's best: France or Italy. The two have faced each other many times, including in the quarter-finals of World Cup 1938 when Italy won 3–1 on their way to being crowned champions. That situation was reversed in the World Cup 1998 quarter-finals, when France beat the Italians on penalties and went on to win the tournament. But things really kicked off in the 2006 World Cup final, when tensions overflowed and Zinedine Zidane saw red for his aforementioned headbutt on Italy's Materazzi. Italy went on to win on penalties, and for both France and Zidane (who was playing his last-ever match) it was a painful end to a glorious era.

◀ Don't make Zinedine Zidane angry. You wouldn't like him when he's angry.

🟥 GERMANY v. NETHERLANDS 🟥

A rivalry born out of Dutch resentment of German occupation during the Second World War, these matches can often seem like wars themselves. Results have swung back and forth, but in two of the biggest World Cup face-offs between the pair, it's the Germans who came out on top. West Germany's 2–1 win over the Dutch in the 1974 World Cup final remains a sore point in the Netherlands, where it's still referred to as 'The Mother of All Defeats'. And, in the round of 16 at World Cup 1990, an especially stormy 2–1 win for the Germans went down in football infamy when the watching world witnessed Frank Rijkaard spit on German striker Rudi Völler – not once, but twice. Nasty.

🔵 BRAZIL v. URUGUAY ⚪

This rivalry is often overlooked, but it's also one of the most intense. These two talented footballing neighbours have battled it out in many a World Cup qualifier and Copa América tie, but surely the apex came in the final round of the 1950 World Cup when Uruguay pulled off a shock 2–1 victory to lift the trophy (see page 89 for the full story). The nation of Brazil was stunned and the match was nicknamed the *Maracanazo* ('the Maracanã Blow'). Brazil didn't get their revenge until 20 years later, when they beat Uruguay 3–1 in the 1970 World Cup semi-final.

🟩 IRAN v. SAUDI ARABIA 🟩

The fact that these two nations have never played a friendly against each other speaks volumes. The two countries have long clashed over political and religious differences, and those differences have spilled over into football – bringing centuries' worth of tension to just 15 on-the-pitch encounters. They haven't met since 2012, but both have made it to Russia, and could even face each other in the round of 16 if both make it through their groups.

MEXICO v. USA

Despite their (unjustified) reputation for not caring about football, the USA have been a part of one of the game's biggest rivalries for over 80 years. As far back as 1934, the Americans shocked the world by beating close neighbours Mexico 4–2 to take North America's only slot at the World Cup in Italy. But it's the period of 2001 to 2016 that today's USA fans hold close to their hearts. During that spell, the Americans racked up an impressive four consecutive 2–0 home wins over the Mexicans, spanning four separate qualification campaigns, and also beat them by the same scoreline at the World Cup in 2002. Cheekily dubbed the *Dos a Cero!* (Spanish for 'two–nil') era by USA fans, it brought with it some of the most hot-blooded encounters in world football – especially for Mexico's Rafael Márquez, who was sent off in two of them.

However, while the USA has won many of the battles, it could be that Mexico is winning the war. The overall head-to-head record points to a hefty lead for the side from south of the border.

◄ Rafael Márquez sees red after headbutting the USA's Cobi Jones in South Korea in 2002.

AUSTRALIA v. JAPAN

Australia have only been members of the Asian confederation for a little over a decade (they were previously part of the Oceania confederation), but this fixture has already become one of the fiercest rivalries on the continent. It all started with a 2006 World Cup group match where Japan took the lead with a controversial goal, infuriating Australian fans. Japan should have doubled their lead when Australia's Tim Cahill blatantly fouled Japan's Yuichi Komano in the box, but the referee didn't see it and this time it was the Japanese who were furious. Their rage only intensified when Cahill scored twice in the final minutes of the match, to secure a 3–1 win and send the Socceroos on the way to their first-ever win at the World Cup. Since then the teams have gone toe-to-toe in front of many a hostile sell-out crowd in huge World Cup qualifying ties, often to decide who wins the group. Japan have had the lion's share of the better results in recent years, most memorably in the 2011 Asian Cup final when Tadanari Lee scored deep into extra-time to banish the ghosts of that 2006 match.

ALGERIA v. EGYPT

When violence broke out at a World Cup 1990 qualifier between these two, supporters rioted in the stands, a player was accused of attacking a fan and the Egyptian team doctor lost an eye. It became known simply as the 'hate match' – but it wasn't the last time tempers would flare between these two. Skip ahead to 2009 and they had to face each other several times in crucial World Cup qualifiers. Ahead of the game in Cairo, Algeria's team bus was stoned and three players were injured – but, incredibly, the Egyptian media claimed that the whole thing had been staged by the Algerians.

ARGENTINA v. ENGLAND

Both these sides have a whole range of sworn rivals to choose from. For England, both Scotland and Germany have provided traditional foes, while Argentina have a long-standing gripe with Brazil.

But England and Argentina sure know how to square up to each other. The rift goes back to the 1966 World Cup quarter-finals, when England won 1–0 with a Geoff Hurst goal that the Argentines insisted was offside. To this day the match is referred to in Argentina as *el robo del siglo* (the theft of the century). The South Americans, however, got their own back. Fast-forward 20 years (past the small matter of the Falklands War between the two countries), and they met again in the quarter-finals of World Cup 1986. Two iconic goals from a certain Diego Maradona gave Argentina a 2–1 victory on their way to winning the tournament. There's also the second-round game at World Cup 1998 where David Beckham was sent off for kicking out at Diego Simeone and became an English national hate figure (see page 114). Oh, and the group match at World Cup 2002 where Beckham scored the only goal and became an English national hero.

IRAN v. USA

The only nations to make our list twice, their rivalry all boils down to one match at World Cup 1998. Against a backdrop of long-standing political turmoil between the two nations, they faced each other in a group match in Lyon. The build-up included a threatened disruption from a terrorist organization, and a refusal from the Iranian Supreme Leader to allow Iran's players to walk towards the Americans for pre-match handshakes. It seemed to have all the ingredients of the ultimate grudge match – but, before kick-off, something remarkable happened. Each Iranian player emerged onto the pitch bearing white roses as a symbol of peace, and the two teams then posed together for a group photo. The world had expected fireworks, but what it got was a striking example of football's power to unite. As for the match itself? Well, that provided almost as big a shock. Iran won 2–1, effectively ditching the States out of the World Cup in the process.

▲ Iranian and American players come together in a memorable show of peace, ahead of their 1998 group match.

THE BEST OF THE REST

Know of any we've missed out? Here are a few other big World Cup rivalries that we couldn't squeeze in . . .

ARGENTINA v. BRAZIL

Maradona or Pelé? Messi or Neymar? Argentina or Brazil? Pick a side!

EL SALVADOR v. HONDURAS

These two have some serious history. Head to page 72 to read all about it.

ENGLAND v. SCOTLAND

The first-ever international football match was played between these two way back in 1872 – and they've been at each other's throats ever since.

ANGOLA v. PORTUGAL

Angola existed under Portuguese colonial rule for nearly 500 years. Portugal beat them when they met at World Cup 2006 . . . but only just.

CROATIA v. SERBIA

Such is the animosity between these two former Yugoslav nations that away fans were banned from both matches when they were drawn together in the 2014 World Cup qualifiers.

GREATEST

The World Cup offers the game's best players the ultimate stage to showcase their skills . . . but it also gives kit manufacturers the chance to show off a bit too. Here are some of the finest bits of clobber to have graced football's number-one tournament.

1. SOVIET UNION (GK) 1962

Black, elegant, intimidating and worn by Lev Yashin. Has a goalkeeper ever looked cooler?

2. PERU 1978

Brilliant white with a red diagonal stripe, Peru's tasty little number from 1978 is, and always will be, a cult classic.

3. ZAIRE 1974

Zaire wore three different tops for three matches in 1974 – all three featuring a massive picture of a leopard mauling a football. This green one with an open-necked yellow collar is our favourite, but all three are a retro kit-lover's dream.

4. DENMARK 1986

Offset stripes weren't routinely seen on football shirts back in 1986, so this jazzy effort was way ahead of its time. Add the black V-neck trim and you've got yourself a kit that football hipsters everywhere still adore over 30 years later.

5. CAMEROON 1990

Another African shirt, another animal. Cameroon – nicknamed the Indomitable Lions – arrived at Italy 1990 in a striking green shirt featuring a yellow, shaggy-maned lion. Couple it with some sharp red shorts, and you've got yourself a bold kit to match the team's playing style.

6. WEST GERMANY 1974

West Germany's iconic 1990 design is a close contender, but sometimes simple is best. With black trim around the neck and cuffs, this is straight to the point and coolness personified.

7. ARGENTINA 1986

The shirt made famous by Diego Maradona in a tournament he dominated. With its simple round neck and pale-blue-and-white stripes, this kit oozes class.

8. FRANCE 1986

France have had many a classic kit, but this one is as stylish as any of them. Has any Frenchman ever looked cooler than Michel Platini did in this? *Non!*

9. CROATIA 1998

At first glance, it might look like a red-and-white chessboard, but as Croatia embarked on their run to the 1998 semis, this one became a real grower. The pattern comes from the Croatian flag and has been a symbol of national pride ever since the country gained independence from Yugoslavia.

10. BRAZIL 1982

Brazil's yellow shirt is one of the most iconic in football, but that wasn't always the case. In the earliest World Cups they played in white, and it wasn't until 1954 that they appeared in the colours we know and love today, thanks to a competition in a newspaper. We're not picking that original design for this rundown, but this beauty from 1982.

11. NETHERLANDS 1974

Great teams need great kits – so step forward this beauty. Orange isn't an easy colour to look good in, but Johan Cruyff and co. certainly managed it.

DID YOU KNOW?

Cruyff's 1974 kit had just two stripes on its sleeves, while his teammates had three. The reason? Cruyff was a Puma man, while this kit was made by Adidas.

1. SOVIET UNION

2. PERU

3. ZAIRE

4. DENMARK

5. CAMEROON

6. WEST GERMANY

7. ARGENTINA

8. FRANCE

9. CROATIA

10. BRAZIL

11. NETHERLANDS

▼ From the greatest kits of the World Cup, to surely one of the most bizarre. This is what Bolivia wore to the very first World Cup in Uruguay in 1930. Intended as a tribute to the hosts, each player sported a bold letter on the front of his shirt, spelling out a message that only made sense when the team posed for the pre-game photo. Unsurprisingly, the idea never caught on.

BELGIUM

Belgium's golden generation have become a regular at the top end of the world rankings, and were the first European side to qualify for Russia. However, after an underwhelming performance at Euro 2016, this star-studded squad has a point to prove.

WORLD CUP NUMBERS

ATTENDED	12
GAMES PLAYED	41
WIN PERCENTAGE	34%
WORLD CUPS WON	0
MILES TO MOSCOW	1,402

MOST CAPS 96	MOST GOALS 30
JAN CEULEMANS	BERNARD VOORHOOF & PAUL VAN HIMST

THEIR GREATEST MOMENT
= 1986 WORLD CUP =

Mexico 1986 was undoubtedly Belgium's greatest World Cup run. The Red Devils saw off hot favourites Soviet Union in the round of 16 and then knocked out Spain on penalties in the quarter-finals. It took eventual winners Argentina to end the Belgian World Cup dream with a 2–0 scoreline in the semi-finals.

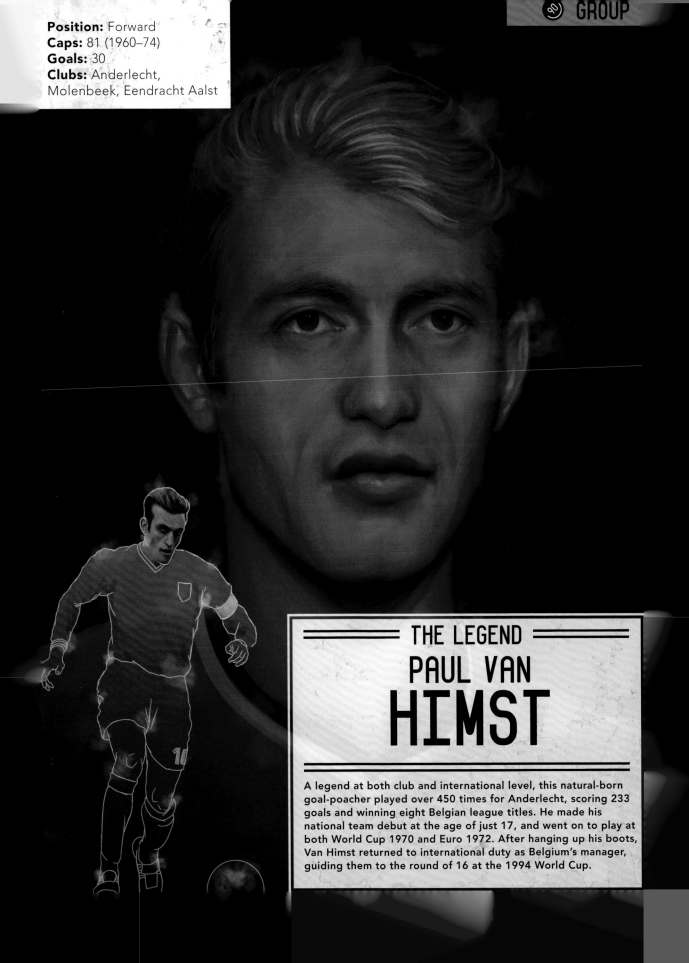

Position: Forward
Caps: 81 (1960–74)
Goals: 30
Clubs: Anderlecht, Molenbeek, Eendracht Aalst

THE LEGEND
PAUL VAN HIMST

A legend at both club and international level, this natural-born goal-poacher played over 450 times for Anderlecht, scoring 233 goals and winning eight Belgian league titles. He made his national team debut at the age of just 17, and went on to play at both World Cup 1970 and Euro 1972. After hanging up his boots, Van Himst returned to international duty as Belgium's manager, guiding them to the round of 16 at the 1994 World Cup.

★ **THE RISING STAR** ★

YANNICK FERREIRA

CARRASCO

Atlético Madrid's flying winger has made a big impact in Spain's La Liga, where his pace and technique have given defenders nightmares on either flank. After appearing in all of Belgium's Euro 2016 matches, he'll expect to be handed a key attacking role for his country in Russia.

DID YOU KNOW?

Belgium played their first official international game in 1904, when they took on France for the Évence Coppée Trophy. The match finished in a 3–3 draw and, because it pre-dated the days of extra-time and penalty shootouts, the trophy was never awarded. It remains unclaimed to this day.

THE RISING STAR ★

MICHAEL AMIR

MURILLO

confident defender plays
ootball in the USA, where he
starred at right-back for MLS
e New York Red Bulls after
ning through the ranks at San
ncisco FC in Panama. After
king his international debut in
endly against Nicaragua in
ch 2016, he quickly became a
member of the Panama team
reached the final of the 2017
a Centroamericana.

DID YOU KNOW?

Upon Panama's qualification
for the 2018 World Cup, President
Juan Carlos Valera immediately
declared a public holiday.
Workers were given the day off
and schools were closed so that
everyone could celebrate the
team's achievement
together.

PANAMA

Arriving in Russia for their first-ever World Cup are Panama. History was made when *La Marea Roja* ('The Red Tide') defeated Costa Rica in the final game of their qualification campaign to pull off one of the major football shocks of the past year.

WORLD CUP NUMBERS

ATTENDED	0
GAMES PLAYED	0
WIN PERCENTAGE	0%
WORLD CUPS WON	0
MILES TO MOSCOW	▶ 6,720

MOST CAPS	140
GABRIEL GÓMEZ	

MOST GOALS	43
LUIS TEJADA	

THEIR GREATEST MOMENT

2009 UNCAF NATIONS CUP

Originally planned to be hosted in Panama City, the tenth UNCAF Nations Cup eventually found a home in Honduras after the Panamanian FA conceded that they wouldn't have a stadium large enough to house the games. That didn't stop the Panama team from scooping the cup for the first time in their history, though, beating Costa Rica 5–3 on penalties in the final.

Position: Forward
Caps: 77 (1963–79)
Goals: 20
Clubs: Deportivo El Granillo, Alianza, Galcasa, Atlético Marte, Universidad de El Salvador, Juventud Olímpica, Provincia de Panamá Metro, Atlético Ciudad de Panamá

THE LEGEND
LUIS ERNESTO
TAPIA

Spotted playing for Panama during a tour of El Salvador as a 17-year-old, Luis Ernesto 'Cascarita' Tapia was quickly signed by Alianza before he even had time to return home. It turned out to be a clever move for both club and player, as Alianza won consecutive league titles in 1965/66 and 1966/67, with Tapia finishing the league's top scorer both times.
In 2010, Panama's training ground was officially renamed Cancha de Entrenamiento Luis Tapia in his honour.

TUNISIA

Tunisia haven't had the best of times at the World Cup over the years. They've qualified four times, but have never gone beyond the group stage and have only ever won one match. They may well have their work cut out for them in 2018, too.

WORLD CUP NUMBERS

ATTENDED	4
GAMES PLAYED	12
WIN PERCENTAGE	8%
WORLD CUPS WON	0
MILES TO MOSCOW	1,830

MOST CAPS 116	MOST GOALS 36
SADOK SASSI	ISSAM JEMÂA

THEIR GREATEST MOMENT

2004 AFRICAN CUP OF NATIONS

After France crashed out of the World Cup in 2002, their manager Roger Lemerre took the reins for Tunisia's attempt to win the African Cup of Nations on home soil. With the pressure well and truly on, the Carthage Eagles responded to the challenge and dominated the tournament, beating Morocco 2–1 in the final. Lemerre, who had previously led France to victory at Euro 2000, became the first manager to win two separate continental tournaments.

Position: Defender
Caps: 105 (1996–2009)
Goals: 7
Clubs: Espérance, Bolton Wanderers, Birmingham City, Southampton

THE LEGEND
RADHI
JAÏDI

After spending 11 years with his hometown club Espérance and winning multiple Tunisian league titles, this towering defender tried his luck in England (where he remains to this day as a coach with Southampton). Many of his greatest moments came in a Tunisia shirt, and he played in both the 2002 and 2006 World Cups, as well as winning the 2004 African Cup of Nations.

★ **THE RISING STAR** ★

NAÏM
SLITI

This Marseille-born attacking midfielder moved to French Ligue 1 side Lille in 2017, and has since gone out on loan to Dijon. A strong dribbler who likes to shoot from distance, Sliti played in all four of Tunisia's matches at the 2017 African Cup of Nations, scoring twice.

DID YOU KNOW?

Tunisia's solitary World Cup win is a significant one. The 3–1 victory over Mexico in 1978 was the first-ever win for an African nation at a World Cup.

★ THE RISING STAR ★

RAHEEM
STERLING

At 23, Sterling already has a £49 million move from Liverpool to Manchester City under his belt. Given that it's the highest fee ever paid for an England player, the tricky midfielder has a lot to live up to – but he's proven his worth with a strong goal return in City colours. So far, he's found goals harder to come by at international level, but that shouldn't prevent him from taking a key role in manager Gareth Southgate's World Cup plans.

DID YOU KNOW?

English non-league side Sheffield FC are the oldest still-active football club on the planet. Not to be confused with the better-known Sheffield United and Sheffield Wednesday, they were founded way back in 1857.

ENGLAND

England came late to the World Cup scene, having not even entered until 1950. They lifted the trophy on home soil in 1966, but the closest they have come since then was an emotional semi-final penalty shootout defeat against West Germany back in 1990.

WORLD CUP NUMBERS

ATTENDED	14
GAMES PLAYED	62
WIN PERCENTAGE	42%
WORLD CUPS WON	★ 1
MILES TO MOSCOW	▶ 1,556

MOST CAPS 🧢 125	MOST GOALS ⚽ 53
PETER SHILTON	WAYNE ROONEY

THEIR GREATEST MOMENT
1966 WORLD CUP

'They think it's all over . . . it is now!' BBC commentator Kenneth Wolstenholme's now-famous words marked Geoff Hurst's third and triumphant goal in the last minutes of extra-time. England had beaten West Germany 4–2 to win the World Cup at a packed Wembley Stadium. Many England sides since have promised much, but none have matched manager Sir Alf Ramsey's achievement in delivering the ultimate trophy.

Position: Midfielder
Caps: 106 (1958–70)
Goals: 49
Clubs: Manchester United, Preston North End, Waterford, Newcastle KB United, Perth Azzurri, Blacktown City

THE LEGEND
BOBBY
CHARLTON

Able to unleash pile-driving shots with both feet, Charlton was a key player in England's 1966 World Cup triumph. At club level he made over 600 appearances for Manchester United, and captained them to their first European Cup victory in 1968, scoring two of United's goals in a historic 4–1 win over Benfica.

CELEBRATION TIME

There's nothing quite like scoring a goal at the World Cup. On a few occasions, the celebrations have been even more memorable than the goals themselves. Here's our timeline of the very best.

PELÉ

BRAZIL v. Italy

Elaborate goal celebrations weren't really a part of football at this point in history, but the sight of Pelé clinging to Jairzinho, one arm aloft, mouth and eyes wide open in glee, remains one of the most iconic World Cup images ever. He'd just scored the opening goal in the final against Italy – a match the Brazilians would go on to win 4–1.

▼ Is there a more recognizable image of sheer footballing joy than a fist-pumping Pelé clinging to Jairzinho in 1970? We doubt it.

1974

JÜRGEN SPARWASSER

EAST GERMANY v. West Germany

East and West Germany met each other for the first and last time in the 1974 group stages – and what an upset it proved to be. East Germany's Sparwasser scored the only goal, and treated the watching world to a little forward roll. Blink and you might miss it, but it was a tiny taster of the flamboyant goal celebrations to come in later years.

◀ Happiness is . . . scoring in the World Cup final. Just like Mario Kempes had just done, here.

1978

MARIO KEMPES
ARGENTINA v. Netherlands

Twice Kempes scored in the final against the Netherlands, and twice he wheeled away, arms outstretched, in absolute delight. The Argentine number ten was unstoppable in this tournament, winning both the Golden Boot (for top scorer) and Golden Ball (for best player), and his celebration was as perfect an embodiment of sheer joy as you're likely to see on a football pitch. Until, that is . . .

1982

MARCO TARDELLI
ITALY v. West Germany

More an outpouring of raw emotion than a celebration, the 'Tardelli Cry' is probably the ultimate expression of how much football can mean to a nation. After scoring Italy's second goal in the final, Tardelli sprinted across the pitch, fists clenched, passionately screaming (some say his own name) with tears streaming down his face. Pure ecstasy!

1986

GORDON STRACHAN
SCOTLAND v. West Germany

Picture the scene: it's the group stages of Mexico 1986, and Strachan has just given Scotland an unlikely lead against the mighty West Germans. He runs to the advertising hoarding to leap joyously towards the fans, but there's just one problem: he's not tall enough to get over them. So he gives up, puts one leg up on the ad board, and shoots a cheeky grin to his teammates. The Scots would go on to lose 2–1 and finish bottom of their group – but Strachan had certainly given the Tartan Army something to smile about.

1990

ROGER MILLA
CAMEROON v. Romania

Cameroon's Roger Milla was 38 years old at the 1990 World Cup, but it didn't stop him from ripping up this tournament with four goals and a big place. After scoring his first goal against Romania, he ran to the corner flag, gyrated his hips and performed a jiggling move that would be replicated by school kids all over the world the following day.

Milla became one of the first footballers to be known for his own trademark goal celebration, and he was also one of the first African players to become a major international star.
He scored a total of five World Cup goals in his career (including one in 1994, at the age of 42!), and celebrated each one with the same joyous dance.

1994

BEBETO
BRAZIL v. Netherlands

Who can forget Bebeto's imaginary-cradle-rocking goal celebration against the Netherlands in the 1994 World Cup quarter-finals? He later revealed that the move was in tribute to his wife, who had just given birth to the couple's third child, Mattheus. And whatever happened to that baby? Now 23, Mattheus turned out to be pretty good at football himself, and in 2016 signed for Portuguese giants Sporting. His dad's celebration lives on in football too, and is often pulled out on the pitch by new fathers to this day.

1998

BRIAN LAUDRUP
DENMARK v. Brazil

What do you do after scoring an equalizing goal against Brazil in a World Cup quarter-final? If you're Brian Laudrup, you slide to the floor, casually prop yourself up on one elbow, and nonchalantly strike a pose that says 'no big deal'. Coolness personified. Laudrup and co. would eventually lose this one 3–2, but went out with their heads held high in what was Denmark's best-ever World Cup performance.

◀ Forget the Lambada, keep your Macarena and don't even mention Gangnam Style. It's time to do the Roger Milla.

◀ Siphiwe Tshabalala (third from the left) throws some of his favourite shapes.

2002

JULIUS AGHAHOWA
NIGERIA v. Sweden

Here's one that would be better suited to the Olympics than the World Cup. After heading the opening goal in this group match, spring-heeled Aghahowa hits a half-dozen or so backflips before ending in a faultless double somersault. Perfect 10! Unfortunately, Nigeria ended up losing this match 2–1 and finishing bottom of the group.

2010

SIPHIWE TSHABALALA
SOUTH AFRICA v. Mexico

As far as significant goals go, they don't come much bigger than the first goal in the first match of the first World Cup your continent has ever hosted. So, it's no wonder Tshabalala wanted to celebrate in style. As Africa rejoiced, the goal hero was joined by four of his teammates to take part in what can only be described as the Macarena, Bafana Bafana-style!

2014

JOHN BROOKS
USA v. Ghana

And so to 2014, and a World Cup where it often felt like slick, choreographed goal celebrations had become the norm. Asamoah Gyan, James Rodríguez, Joel Campbell – they were all at it. But sometimes the best celebration of all is just a guy, scoring a goal, and looking like he absolutely cannot believe what has just happened. And for that, you can't beat John Brooks's response to scoring a late winner to help send the USA through to the knockout stage.

HOW THE WEB WOULD HAVE REACTED . . .

Sadly, social media wasn't around when many of the World Cup's most memorable moments happened. Here's how we reckon a few of them might have gone down.

SUPREME EFFORT

You knew to expect glitz and glamour from the opening ceremony of 1994. It's what the USA does best. And what could be more glamorous than Diana Ross striding along to 'I'm Coming Out' and slotting a penalty past a flailing keeper? Unfortunately, she shanked it wide, bless her. But the goal frame still did its job and burst apart anyway.

DIANA ROSS SKILLS, TRICKS & GOALS

0:15 / 7:45

 PASSING THE BALL

 MOVING FORWARD WITH THE BALL

 DRIBBLING PAST THE DEFENDER

 CRUYFF TURN

TURN OF THE CENTURY

A moment of pure magic from 1974, as Dutch legend Johan Cruyff pulls out the piece of trickery that carries his name to this day. Jan Olsson, the Swedish defender on the receiving end, almost falls over – partly due to shock, and partly due to getting turned completely inside out.

BLUE MONDAY

Two extremes of football's emotion, shown by two Italians. Marco Tardelli wheels away in pure, unrestrained joy after putting his side 2–0 up against West Germany in the 1982 final. And a devastated Roberto Baggio hangs his head after blazing his penalty over the bar to hand Brazil the trophy in 1994. If pictures can paint a thousand words, it's proven by these two.

FRIDAY NIGHT

MONDAY MORNING

WHEN IT'S BEEN AN HOUR AND NO ONE'S RESPONDED ON THE GROUP CHAT.

THE CRYING GAME

It's the semi-final of 1990, and England's Paul Gascoigne, maverick and talisman, is booked for a poorly timed lunge on West Germany's Thomas Berthold, instantly ruling himself out of a potential World Cup final. Cue tears of despair from Gazza, and the moment that defined the tournament for a whole nation.

DEFENDER DISTRACTION

Preparing to face a Brazilian free-kick at 2–0 down during the 1974 World Cup, Zaire defender Joseph Mwepu Ilunga breaks from the wall and blasts the ball into the distance. It turned out, though, that this was no mistake.

Mwepu Ilunga

Rest of the Zaire team

Head to page 114 to find out more about Ilunga's moment of madness.

POLAND

Poland's glory years of finishing third at both the 1974 and 1982 World Cups are a long time ago now – but they topped their qualifying group with a swagger, scoring 13 goals in their final three games. Expect them to be dangerous in their first World Cup since 2006.

WORLD CUP NUMBERS

ATTENDED	7
GAMES PLAYED	31
WIN PERCENTAGE	48%
WORLD CUPS WON	0
MILES TO MOSCOW	715

MOST CAPS 102	MOST GOALS 51
MICHAL ŻEWLAKOW	ROBERT LEWANDOWSKI

THEIR GREATEST MOMENT

= THE LAST GAME =

Uniquely, our pick for Poland's greatest moment is a friendly match. On 27 August 1939, as the shadow of the Second World War hung over Europe, the Poles squared up to one of the best teams on the planet. Hungary had finished runners-up at the previous year's World Cup in France, and were expected to dominate the game. However, the Poles recorded a historic victory, winning 4–2. War broke out just four days later, and Poland wouldn't play another international until 1946. To this day, the match is still famous in Poland as 'The Last Game'.

Position: Winger
Caps: 100 (1971–84)
Goals: 45
Clubs: Stal Mielec, Lokeren, Atlante, Polonia Hamilton

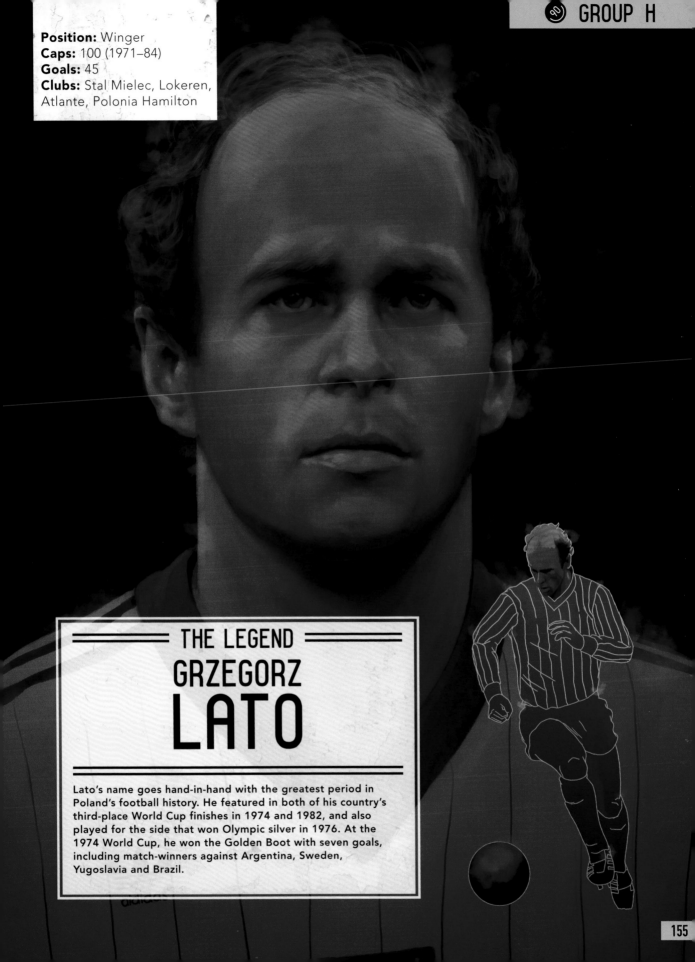

THE LEGEND
GRZEGORZ
LATO

Lato's name goes hand-in-hand with the greatest period in Poland's football history. He featured in both of his country's third-place World Cup finishes in 1974 and 1982, and also played for the side that won Olympic silver in 1976. At the 1974 World Cup, he won the Golden Boot with seven goals, including match-winners against Argentina, Sweden, Yugoslavia and Brazil.

THE RISING STAR ★

PIOTR
ZIELINSKI

briefly featuring at Euro 2016,
r-old Zieliński went on to
sh himself as a regular at the
of the Poland midfield during
orld Cup qualifiers. Based in
is form at Empoli while on loan
dinese earned him a €16
move to Napoli in the summer
6. His Champions League
ence with the Serie A giants
stand him in good stead when
es to taking the field at the
t tournament of them all.

DID YOU KNOW?

Polish goal hero
Robert Lewandowski has
sport in his blood. His father was
a judo champion and lower-league
footballer, his mother is a former
volleyball player and his sister has
played international U21
volleyball for Poland.

★ THE RISING STAR ★

KEITA BALDÉ

DIAO

Despite being born in Spain, 23-year-old Baldé Diao has chosen to play for his father's nation of birth, Senegal. After spending time in the Barcelona youth academy, he secured a move to Italian side Lazio where he became a first-team regular. Having now moved to Monaco for a reported €30 million, big things are expected of this confident striker.

DID YOU KNOW?

When Senegal forward Sadio Mané moved from Southampton to Liverpool for £35 million in 2016, he became the most expensive African footballer of all time. That record has since been broken by another Liverpool player – Egypt's Mohamed Salah, who went to Anfield from Roma for a reported £39 million.

SENEGAL

Sixteen years on from their debut appearance, the Lions of Teranga are roaring back into the World Cup. Can this new generation match the class of 2002, who went all the way to the quarter-finals?

WORLD CUP NUMBERS

ATTENDED	1
GAMES PLAYED	5
WIN PERCENTAGE	40%
WORLD CUPS WON	0
MILES TO MOSCOW	4,051

MOST CAPS 99	MOST GOALS 29
HENRI CAMARA	HENRI CAMARA

THEIR GREATEST MOMENT
= 2002 WORLD CUP =

Senegal couldn't have asked for a better World Cup debut. No one gave them a chance in the opening game against defending champions France, but Papa Bouba Diop made the world sit up and take notice when he scored the game's only goal. Bruno Metsu's side went on to draw with Denmark and Uruguay before knocking out Sweden in the round of 16. It took an extra-time goal from Turkey in the quarter-finals to finally end their World Cup dream.

Position: Forward
Caps: 99 (1999–2008)
Goals: 29
Clubs: RC Strasbourg, Neuchâtel Xamax, Grasshopper Club Zürich, Sedan, Wolverhampton Wanderers, Celtic, Southampton, Wigan Athletic, West Ham United, Stoke City, Sheffield United, Atromitos, Panetolikos (twice), Kalloni, Lamia, Apollon Smyrni, Ionikos

THE LEGEND
HENRI
CAMARA

He scored more goals and won more caps than any other Senegalese player in history, and he also scored both goals in the 2–1 win over Sweden that took his nation into the 2002 World Cup quarter-finals. This man-of-many-clubs played for teams all over Europe, including a short-but-sweet spell with Wolves in England during which he scored six goals in nine games at the end of the 2003/04 season. Camara eventually finished his career in the Greek Super League.

COLOMBIA

Colombia returned to the world stage in 2014 after a 16-year absence, and went all the way to the quarter-finals. With a team built around the supremely talented James Rodríguez, *La Tricolor* will fancy their chances of doing even better this time around.

WORLD CUP NUMBERS

ATTENDED	5
GAMES PLAYED	18
WIN PERCENTAGE	39%
WORLD CUPS WON	0
MILES TO MOSCOW	6,435

MOST CAPS	111
CARLOS VALDERRAMA	

MOST GOALS	28
RADAMEL FALCAO	

THEIR GREATEST MOMENT

=2001 COPA AMÉRICA=

The year 2001 threw up one of the most dramatic championships in Copa América history. Security concerns in the days prior to the tournament led to it being cancelled, only to be reinstated with just days to go. Amid the disarray, hosts Colombia dominated every stage of the competition, winning all three group matches and marching all the way to the final against Mexico. Iván Córdoba's headed goal proved to be enough to give his nation its first (and so far only) major trophy.

Position: Midfielder
Caps: 111 (1985–98)
Goals: 11
Clubs: Unión Magdalena, Millonarios, Deportivo Cali (twice), Montpellier, Real Valladolid, Independiente Medellín, Atlético Junior, Tampa Bay Mutiny (twice), Miami Fusion, Colorado Rapids

THE LEGEND
CARLOS VALDERRAMA

Known as much for his tight, precise passing as his mop of wild blond curls, the legendary Colombian number ten was a true playmaker, forever taking risks to provide his teammates with countless goalscoring opportunities. Twice named South American Footballer of the Year, *El Pibe* ('The Kid') made over 600 club-level appearances in a career that spanned two decades, earning himself the captain's armband at three successive World Cups.

THE RISING STAR ★

DAVINSON SANCHEZ

...owerful central defender
...22 just two days before the
... Cup kicks off, so will be
...g he's done enough in his
...eason at Tottenham Hotspur
...ebrate his birthday in Russia.
... paid a reported £42 million
...g him to White Hart Lane,
...he impressed in the Dutch
...ight with Ajax.

DID YOU KNOW?

At Chile 1962, Colombia's Marcos Coll became the only player ever to score directly from a corner kick at a World Cup. His incredible strike came in a 4–4 draw with the Soviet Union, and earned him the nickname *El Olímpico* (after the term 'Olympic goal', referring to a goal from a corner).

★ **THE RISING STAR** ★

YOSUKE

IDEGUCHI

Yosuke Ideguchi's stunning 84th-minute goal against Australia in the qualifiers not only booked Japan's place in Russia, but secured his own status as a national hero. At just 21 years old, this speedy box-to-box midfielder has already won the J.League's 'Rookie of the Year' award with Gamba Osaka and looks odds-on to play a big part at the World Cup. Look out for his long-passing ability and knack for creating chances.

DID YOU KNOW?

Japan's nickname comes from their blue kit, but why don't Samurai Blue play in the red and white of their flag? It's all down to superstition. Japan wore blue at the 1936 Summer Olympics, where they reached the quarter-finals. Since then, blue has been considered lucky.

JAPAN

They're one of the powerhouses of Asian football, but it wasn't until 1998 that Japan qualified for their first World Cup. Since then, they have been ever-presents, but progression beyond the round of 16 still eludes them.

WORLD CUP NUMBERS

ATTENDED	5
GAMES PLAYED	17
WIN PERCENTAGE	24%
WORLD CUPS WON	0
MILES TO MOSCOW	4,652

MOST CAPS	152
YASUHITO ENDO	

MOST GOALS	80
KUNISHIGE KAMAMOTO	

THEIR GREATEST MOMENT
= 2002 WORLD CUP =

While Japan has won the AFC Asian Cup four times, it's the 2002 World Cup that truly signalled Samurai Blue's arrival on the global stage. As co-hosts with South Korea, they packed out stadiums with enthusiastic fans who had genuine dreams of World Cup glory. In the end, it wasn't to be (they crashed out in the round of 16, losing to Turkey), but in many ways 2002 was the moment when the world truly took notice of Japan's ability to become a football force.

Position: Forward
Caps: 84 (1964–77)
Goals: 80
Club: Yanmar Diesel

THE LEGEND
KUNISHIGE
KAMAMOTO

At the age of just 20, this prolific goalscorer was plucked from his university side to play for his country at the 1964 Olympics, and went on to become the first major superstar of Japanese football. At the 1968 Olympics in Mexico he was the tournament's top scorer with seven goals, and he was Japan's Footballer of the Year seven times.

ULTIMATE WORLD CUP XI

Considering the sheer number of great players to have graced the World Cup stage, this wasn't easy. We've selected our all-time World Cup starting XI: a team with greatness running through its veins and international experience at its core.

Each member of this side is special in their own right. If you combined all of their on-the-pitch smarts, you'd have the greatest footballing brain there ever was. Who are they?

It's time to find out . . .

GOALKEEPER
LEV YASHIN

Soviet Union

How could we possibly put anyone else between the sticks? We've already sung his praises earlier in this book, and for good reason. He played in four World Cups, won the Euros, won the Olympics, won the Ballon d'Or and – legend has it – saved over 150 penalty kicks. Put simply, you'd have to be some striker to get past the 'Black Spider' and, with the World Cup taking place on Russian soil for the first time, it's fitting that the first name on our team sheet is one of Moscow's very own.

INTERNATIONAL CAPS: *78*
WORLD CUP RECORD:
Quarter-finals in 1958
Quarter-finals in 1962
Fourth place in 1966
Quarter-finals in 1970

RIGHT–BACK
LILIAN THURAM

France

All the best football teams have a bit of rivalry in the dressing room . . . so, we've selected the only full-back who can rival Roberto Carlos's thighs! When you think of Thuram, you might not think of goals. However, when he did score them, they were often pivotal. Both of his international goals came in the 1998 World Cup semi-final against Croatia – a match France won 2–1. The French went on to win the trophy that year on their own home soil, and Thuram was a massive part of a defence that conceded just two goals along the way. He went on to be a defensive rock for France for another ten years, becoming the most-capped French player of all time.

INTERNATIONAL CAPS: *142*
INTERNATIONAL GOALS: *2*
WORLD CUP RECORD:
Winner in 1998
Group stage in 2002
Runner-up in 2006

LEFT-BACK
ROBERTO CARLOS

Brazil

Who else would you have on free-kicks? His left foot produced a bullet of a shot that travelled at 105 miles per hour. Not bad for a guy standing at five-foot-six! With thighs like tree trunks and the tenacity of a bull, Roberto Carlos reached the final with Brazil in 1998 and, four years later, went one better and bagged himself a winners' medal. When you play at left-back in a team that includes players like Ronaldinho, Ronaldo and Rivaldo, and still manage to stand out, it pretty much says it all.

INTERNATIONAL CAPS: *125*
INTERNATIONAL GOALS: *11*
WORLD CUP RECORD:
Runner-up in 1998
Winner in 2002
Quarter-finals in 2006

▼ As both a player and a manager, Franz Beckenbauer was a winner. Here he is after guiding West Germany to glory in 1990.

CENTRE-BACK
FRANZ BECKENBAUER (C)

West Germany

Der Kaiser played the game at his own pace, with a positional sense that thwarted even the world's best strikers. This was a no-nonsense defender with a distinctly high pain threshold to match. Despite dislocating his shoulder during the semi-final against Italy at the 1970 World Cup, Beckenbauer somehow managed to play on with his arm in a sling. Now, that's the type of determination we want to see in our team!

He wasn't done there, either. After retirement, instead of relaxing and piling on the pounds like some ex-pros (who we won't name!), Franz went on to win the World Cup in 1990 as Germany's manager. A true leader, and therefore the captain of our team.

INTERNATIONAL CAPS: *103*
INTERNATIONAL GOALS: *14*
WORLD CUP RECORD:
Runner-up in 1966
Third place in 1970
Winner in 1974
Winner in 1990 (as manager)

CENTRE-BACK
BOBBY MOORE

England

When Pelé name-checks you as one of the greatest defenders ever to grace the game, you know you're not bad. The late Bobby Moore epitomized the spirit of England's 1966 World Cup-winning side. With a mixture of grit, determination and a born understanding of the game, Moore played football the way it was meant to be played. He even grabbed himself an assist in the World Cup final with a quickly taken free-kick. Not too shabby for a centre-back.

INTERNATIONAL CAPS: *108*
INTERNATIONAL GOALS: *2*
WORLD CUP RECORD:
Quarter-finals in 1962
Winner in 1966
Quarter-finals in 1970

RIGHT-WING
DIEGO MARADONA

Argentina

A controversial player as far as World Cups go, especially if you're English. However, for all of the controversy that comes with the package, there's no denying he could light up a football pitch like no one else. He's a player who could change the game at a flick of a switch and could power through defences seemingly at will. Some of the greatest players at club level have struggled to make an impact at the World Cup. Not Diego . . . he thrived!

INTERNATIONAL CAPS: *91*
INTERNATIONAL GOALS: *34*
WORLD CUP RECORD:
Second round in 1982
Winner in 1986
Runner-up in 1990
Second round in 1994
Quarter-finals in 2010
(as manager)

CENTRE-MIDFIELD
XAVI

Spain

A true footballing wizard, with the ability to create space out of thin air. Xavi simply does not lose the ball. He was instrumental in Spain's 2010 World Cup triumph and became the embodiment of their 'tiki-taka' playing style, finishing the tournament with a breath-taking pass-completion rate of 91 per cent. Put Xavi in any football team and he'd be its metronome, dictating the pace of the game from one box to the other – and that's why he's in ours.

INTERNATIONAL CAPS: *133*
INTERNATIONAL GOALS: *13*
WORLD CUP RECORD:
Quarter-finals in 2002
Second round in 2006
Winner in 2010
Group stage in 2014

CENTRE-MIDFIELD
ZINEDINE ZIDANE

France

Lining up alongside the steadiness of Xavi, we have the brilliant Zinedine Zidane. Zizou had a way of making the game seem effortless. Watching him, you got the impression that his approach would be the same whether he was having a kick-about with his mates or playing in a World Cup final (he played in two, by the way). His cool manner, combined with his passion for the game and sheer ability to pick out an impossible pass or score from any angle, made him the best of his generation. For a Zidane masterclass, look no further than his performance in the final of 1998, in which he tore Brazil apart and scored two devastating headed goals.

INTERNATIONAL CAPS: *108*
INTERNATIONAL GOALS: *31*
WORLD CUP RECORD:
Winner in 1998
Group stage in 2002
Runner-up in 2006

◄ Bobby Moore, England's captain and defensive linchpin, goes up for one of many headers during the 1966 final.

LEFT-WING
JOHAN CRUYFF
Netherlands

If you're looking for your side to play beautiful football, then you should probably pick the player who epitomizes 'total football'. Oh, and it might also help if that player has a move named after him. It can only be one man: Johan Cruyff. Whether playing on the left or the right, Cruyff left defenders in his wake time and time again. But his World Cup pinnacle came in 1974 when, on the way to the final, he pulled out his famous 'Cruyff Turn', bamboozling Swedish defender Jan Olsson. To this day, it's a move that players all over the planet attempt to copy, from grassroots pitches to the international stage. It would turn out to be Cruyff's only World Cup, but before retiring from the international game he helped his nation reach Argentina 1978, where his countrymen would once again go all the way to the final.

INTERNATIONAL CAPS: *48*
INTERNATIONAL GOALS: *33*
WORLD CUP RECORD:
Runner-up in 1974

STRIKER
PELÉ
 Brazil

How could he not make our ultimate XI? Arguably the best striker of all time, Pelé played in four World Cups and is the only player to have won three (his first at just 17 years old). By the time of his fourth World Cup, he was the best player in the world, and that 1970 Brazil World Cup team is often considered to be the best football team ever. He was pivotal in their victorious route to the final, scoring four times and setting up Carlos Alberto's famous goal against Italy (a goal that has been called the greatest-ever team goal). To this day, he remains Brazil's record goalscorer, and probably the most famous footballer in history. Suffice to say, he goes straight into our attack.

INTERNATIONAL CAPS: *92*
INTERNATIONAL GOALS: *77*
WORLD CUP RECORD:
Winner in 1958
Winner in 1962
Group stage in 1966
Winner in 1970

◄ Pelé embarks on a mazy solo run during Brazil's 2–0 group-stage win over Bulgaria at World Cup 1966.

THE BEST OF THE REST

Who did we miss? Here are some of the names that might jostle for a place on our subs' bench.

Gordon Banks

England's 1966 World Cup-winning keeper is perhaps best known for the borderline miraculous save he made from a Pelé header in the 1970 group stages.

Lothar Matthäus

The only outfield player to appear in five different World Cup tournaments, Matthäus was the rock at the centre of the German team for 20 years and captained them to victory at Italy 1990.

Garrincha

Surely one of the best dribblers ever, Garrincha was a World Cup winner with Brazil in both 1958 and 1962 (and was both joint-top scorer and player of the tournament at the latter).

Miroslav Klose

The World Cup's all-time top scorer with 16 goals spread across four World Cups with Germany (including the victorious 2014 side).

Ronaldo

Snapping at Klose's heels on the World Cup scoring charts, the Brazilian icon grabbed 15 in three World Cups, and is second only to Pelé as Brazil's all-time top hitman.

Just Fontaine

This Moroccan-born frontman only played 21 times for France, but scored an incredible 30 goals and was top scorer at Sweden 1958.

STRIKER
FERENC PUSKÁS
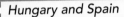
Hungary and Spain

We finish our front line with this absolute warrior. Puskás was certainly not the type of striker who you'd see diving or rolling around on the ground. On the contrary, he played for Hungary in the 1954 final with a hairline fracture on his ankle – and still scored. That was one of four goals he notched up during the Mighty Magyars' run to the tournament's showpiece match in Bern. Unusually, Puskás would go on to take Spanish nationality and played three times for Spain at the 1962 World Cup – but, on the international stage, it's undoubtedly his appearances in a Hungary shirt for which he's best known. He sadly died in 2006, but his name lives on through the Puskás Award, an accolade that, fittingly, goes to the scorer of the 'most beautiful' goal of each year. In total, he scored 84 times in 85 Hungary matches. If your team needs a goal, this is your man.

INTERNATIONAL CAPS: *85*
(plus 4 for Spain)
INTERNATIONAL GOALS: *84*
WORLD CUP RECORD:
Runner-up in 1954 (with Hungary)
Group stage in 1962 (with Spain)

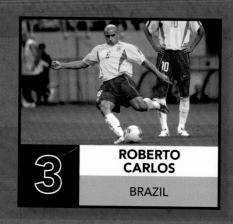

3 ROBERTO CARLOS

BRAZIL

5 FRANZ BECKENBAUER (C)

WEST GERMANY

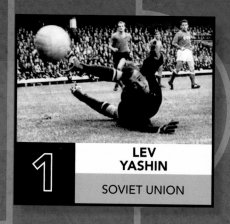

1 LEV YASHIN

SOVIET UNION

6 BOBBY MOORE

ENGLAND

2 LILIAN THURAM

FRANCE

7
JOHAN CRUYFF
NETHERLANDS

8
ZINEDINE ZIDANE
FRANCE

9
FERENC PUSKÁS
HUNGARY & SPAIN

4
XAVI
SPAIN

10
PELÉ
BRAZIL

11
DIEGO MARADONA
ARGENTINA

90

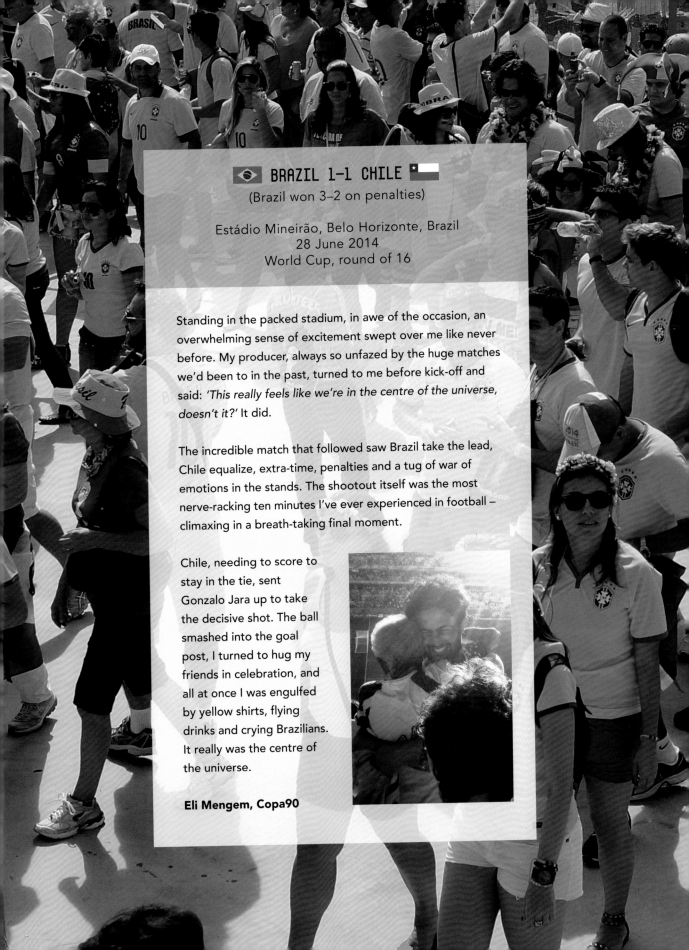

🇧🇷 BRAZIL 1–1 CHILE 🇨🇱
(Brazil won 3–2 on penalties)

Estádio Mineirão, Belo Horizonte, Brazil
28 June 2014
World Cup, round of 16

Standing in the packed stadium, in awe of the occasion, an overwhelming sense of excitement swept over me like never before. My producer, always so unfazed by the huge matches we'd been to in the past, turned to me before kick-off and said: *'This really feels like we're in the centre of the universe, doesn't it?'* It did.

The incredible match that followed saw Brazil take the lead, Chile equalize, extra-time, penalties and a tug of war of emotions in the stands. The shootout itself was the most nerve-racking ten minutes I've ever experienced in football – climaxing in a breath-taking final moment.

Chile, needing to score to stay in the tie, sent Gonzalo Jara up to take the decisive shot. The ball smashed into the goal post, I turned to hug my friends in celebration, and all at once I was engulfed by yellow shirts, flying drinks and crying Brazilians. It really was the centre of the universe.

Eli Mengem, Copa90

Thanks to Jo Simmons and Barry Flanigan for their invaluable support throughout the project.

Photography credits